HEALING TAPESTRY

A Memoir of Divine Guidance

THE
HEALING
TAPESTRY

A Memoir of Divine Guidance

DAVID W. MCCLURE

DEDICATION

I dedicate this book to my beloved soulmate, companion, and wife, Donna, without whom this book would only be a hope and a dream on the back shelf of my mind. I also dedicate this book to all the trailblazers who carried forward the unifying threads of possibility, especially the founders known as the Mother and Father of Unity, Myrtle and Charles Fillmore.

There is a unifying thread that runs through every life. We experience this thread in two distinct ways that are woven into the fabric of every soul. The healing thread is first experienced through the heart (feeling). The guiding thread is known to us through our head (thinking). Thus, heart and head are the mother and father of all creation, all healing, all guidance, and all transformation. When these two team up, get ready for infinite possibilities!

TABLE OF CONTENTS

INTRODUCTION

In the beginning were the threads. And the threads were God. — David 1:1

 While I was living in Australia in the mid-1960s, I took a few days off from the ministry I was serving in Sydney to visit the very heart and center of the continent, a place called Ayers Rock, or as the Aboriginals call it, *Uluru.* The Australian Aboriginals are considered among the most primitive people on our planet. Their culture is one of the oldest if not the oldest in the world, dating back more than 65,000 years, according to the National Museum of Australia. There are many archaeological sites throughout the country where the long history of these indigenous peoples can be found.

At Uluru, I saw amazing cave drawings that I was told were the first form of guidance used by the Aboriginals. Living as they did in a region the Australians call the "back of beyond," a sense of direction and purpose was essential. For example, they would draw a picture of an animal on the wall of the cave, then leave the cave and seem to be guided through the surrounding desert to the actual animal that would feed them and their families. We might think of these people as among the first to use visualizing and treasure mapping to attract their good.

Aside from the drawings of animals such as kangaroos and wallabies, there were other curious drawings in these caves. I saw what appeared to be nothing more than concentric circles. A guide said the circles were a way of giving direction to those who gaze upon them. They primarily represent the interconnectedness of all life. The center represents our innermost selves, and the

1

outermost circles represent the universe. The middle circle represents our connection to other people, and the other two circles represent our connection to nature. He concluded by saying, "Basically, this is the Aboriginal symbol for God."

The full impact of this revelation did not hit home with me at the time. But thinking about it in recent days, I realized this might very well be the starting point of the original thread of all life—what we have come to know as God by many names. It is now my contention that from this single thread there began unfurling two distinct strands, each with its own purpose, a healing thread and a guiding thread. These two, entwined and eternally connected as one, set about creating all life on planet Earth. In my mind, I began to ask: *Is this where all life on the planet began?*

The Original Thread

I have been an ordained Unity minister for more than 60 years, and my wife, Donna, for 23 years. We belong to a global, inclusive, spiritual community that offers life-changing resources to help people of all faiths or no faith apply positive, practical principles in their everyday lives. Application of these principles brings healing, guidance, prosperity, and transformation into the lives of thousands living here on planet Earth.

The original logo for Unity was a winged globe. I am beginning to wonder: *Were these wings intended to represent the feminine and masculine threads of all creation? Could they possibly represent the mother and father of all life, which, when working together, lift all of life to a higher level of expression?*

Unity started for me with an affirmation that to this day is used in many Unity ministries to open Sunday services and to open hearts and minds to unlimited possibilities. *There is only One Presence and One Power in the Universe, God the Good, Omnipotent.* These were the first words I heard when I walked into the Unity Church of Truth in Toronto, Canada. I was 7 years old. Since then, I've narrowed those words into one simple name: the unifying thread. This is and always has been the fundamental principle of Unity.

Unity started with the concept of oneness. From there, two intelligent and deeply curious individuals began their quest for truth and understanding, hoping to find their way to a deeper sense of all they were created to be. These curious ones, a woman and a man, began to discover for and within themselves the unfolding of this unifying thread. They began to comprehend the basic premise and foundation of all life—what life is and always has been—unity.

The Bible puts it this way: "In the beginning, God ..." (Genesis 1:1). You might say that all life starts from wholeness, perfection, and completion. Everything begins and ends with unity. Everything is connected, woven together.

I believe all life and all creation came from this single, unifying thread of oneness. And from this One evolved a dynamic, creative process where the One unwound itself into two distinct expressions or threads. From these emerged a magnificent tapestry of all life, including all the beings that have ever walked and are walking the earth today. All are connected.

This one thread, which is the source and unifier of all there is, involved itself in humanity through a creative process utilizing both the feminine/heart and masculine/mind. The feminine and masculine to which I am referring have nothing to do with human gender. We all have qualities of both. These two threads continue to manifest in unlimited shapes and forms. They have guided and healed us and so many others. These threads walk with us today and every day. And it is because of these two threads that I have written this book.

3

The Healing Thread

Many students of Unity—we call ourselves *students* because there is no ultimate graduation in life; there is always more to learn and to become—might say that Unity as we know it got its start about 2,000 years ago. An event happened that introduced a powerful thread with new and astonishing possibilities. As this thread began to unwind, it began to impact, transform, and change millions of lives, including ours as we are living it today.

That event was the birth of Jesus of Nazareth. With him came not only a teaching that was life-changing but a way of being, a way of life that was practical, usable, and accessible to everyone. Jesus' life became a model that would upgrade the way millions lived their lives while residing here on planet Earth, especially in the two major areas of healing and guidance.

Many of those who came under the influence and inspiration of Jesus went on to teach and demonstrate his basic tenets and principles with astonishing results.

Jesus was a living example of healing and guidance. He demonstrated that a unifying thread joined together all humankind and the many forms life takes into a spiritual reality that is our true identity. He taught that this thread is accessed through one or both of the dual threads—the heart and/or the mind. We reach the one thread through a combination of our feeling and thinking.

An important piece of Jesus' healing thread revealed itself in the 1800s to a spiritual teacher named Emma Curtis Hopkins. Hopkins passed her understanding along to many, including a married couple, Myrtle and Charles Fillmore of Kansas City, Missouri. Here's what Charles Fillmore had to say about Hopkins: "She is undoubtedly the most successful teacher in the world. In many instances those who enter her classes [as] confirmed invalids come out at the end of the course perfectly well. Her very presence heals, and those who listen are filled with new life. Never before on this planet have such words of burning Truth been so eloquently spoken through a woman."

The Fillmores—Charles in his early 30s, Myrtle nine years older—found themselves in the throes of significant and serious healing predicaments.

I want to tell you their story in some detail, partly because my wife Donna and I have spent our lives in Unity, the spiritual movement the Fillmores founded, and also because the healing principles they taught have played a profound role in our own healing journeys.

'I Am a Child of God ...'

Myrtle Fillmore suffered with tuberculosis (TB), considered perhaps the most fatal disease of her time. Contracting tuberculosis (known as consumption) in the mid-1880s to early 1900s was a death sentence—and a drawn-out one at that. Sufferers of the infectious disease, which typically attacks the lungs, had an average of three years to live. Those years would be filled with coughing and chest pains.

This combined with the long-term effects of malaria led Myrtle's doctors to abandon hope for her healing and give her mere months to live. She was 40 years of age with two young sons at the time.

Facing down her death sentence, Myrtle gathered what strength she could muster and, together with her husband Charles, began looking for some thread, some hope to hang onto, any strand of hope or encouragement that might shift Myrtle's dire diagnosis.

Eventually, seemingly out of the blue, a thread of possibility revealed itself. This was a strand that ultimately led them to attend a lecture one night in 1886 in Kansas City, Missouri.

There is a verse in the Book of Proverbs that goes: "Keep your heart with all diligence, for out of it are the issues of life" (Proverbs 4:23). I understand this to mean that when we listen to our heart, a new portal within us opens to the universal field of infinite possibilities (another name for the unifying thread) and great

5

healing has a chance to be born. (By the way, the Universal Field of Infinite Possibilities (UFIP) is my newest name for God!)

The lecturer that night was a man named Dr. E.B. Weeks, a student of the aforementioned Emma Curtis Hopkins. As Myrtle listened, she heard words that went directly to her heart. These words formed what would become a single strand of healing that was, from that moment on, destined to change her life and the lives of millions all over the world. Here then is the thread that was revealed to her that night:

I am a child of God, and therefore I do not inherit sickness.

Consider the implications of these words. Myrtle, having given up almost every hope of restoration, was astonished to hear words that resonated immediately and repeatedly within her. Though these words directly contradicted her current thinking and feeling, something shifted within her soul, and she began to enter a new and unexplored part of her being. A healing portal had opened within her. The healing thread began to wend its way into her heart and on through her body and out into her relationships.

She went home from the lecture with these words ringing in her heart and mind and began repeating them to herself: *I am a child of God, and therefore I do not inherit sickness.*

If she was indeed a child of God, then this would mean she was no longer attached to the family gene but rather to a divine gene, the unifying gene, one of a higher, deeper reality that carried with it the powerful possibility of healing and wholeness.

Bolstered by this new revelation, this new thought, she began to claim her divine inheritance and found herself stepping into the same healing flow that had been introduced and articulated some 2,000 years ago by Jesus and was now being echoed by E.B. Weeks in his lecture. It was at that moment the heart of the Unity movement was born.

This healing thread not only works within the body but moves out to embrace all of our relationships to strengthen and enrich them.

Stunned by his wife's improvement, Charles Fillmore began experimenting with the same healing ideas and principles and experienced substantial healing of a withered leg from a childhood accident.

Here began this couple's search to understand and explain their newfound health, followed by their historic decision to dedicate their lives to helping others discover their own healing and guiding threads. Myrtle, having overcome her death sentence, lived to the age of 86 and Charles to just shy of 94.

Know that with every day, even as you read this book, this healing thread surrounds, embraces, and now intertwines with your life and mine. It remains available, accessible, visible, and powerful, whenever and wherever it is called upon, acknowledged, and affirmed. The healing thread is at work in your body and in your relationships with others to heal and harmonize, to enhance and transform.

Threads of Heart and Mind

It wasn't long after the Fillmores began to manifest dramatic changes in their own physical bodies that they realized their discovery, although very personal, belonged to everyone on earth. Their guidance was to pass it on to as many people as they could reach. The healing thread was about to do a mighty work.

In 1889, Myrtle was guided to begin gathering friends and acquaintances at her home to pray, and within a year she created what was called the Society of Silent Help. The group was renamed the Society of Silent Unity in 1891. Ultimately, a prayer and healing ministry called Silent Unity® was developed, answering prayer requests by letter and later by telephone. Today, prayer associates still pray with callers on the telephone, but nearly half the 1.3 million prayer requests each year are submitted online.

The Fillmores also began publishing a magazine, first called *Modern Thought* and then *Unity Magazine*®, which now circulates under the name *Spirituality & Health*®: *A Unity Publication*. Through the years they added more magazines including the flagship *Daily Word*®, books, and pamphlets—creating a publishing house for spiritual material. They intended it for people in any church, of any faith.

Charles Fillmore studied world religions and the scripture of other faiths. It was then that the second of these two branches of the unifying thread—the guiding thread, the thread of head or mind—revealed itself to complete the unity in Unity.

Myrtle, in an article called "How I Found Health" for *Unity Magazine* in 1897, wrote: "Life has to be guided and directed by man's inner intelligence in making all forms."

Charles reached a point where he wanted nothing less than an immediate and firsthand experience of the guiding thread— the one presence and one power of the universe. He wanted to touch the universal field of unlimited possibilities. After studying many teachings that seemed to confuse him more, he wrote, "I said to myself, 'In this babel I will go to headquarters. If I am Spirit and this God they talk so much about is Spirit, we can somehow communicate, or the whole thing is a fraud.'"

Soon Charles found himself awakening early every morning and spending great amounts of time in still and silent meditation. He said he loved to pray before the world awakened and started thinking its worldly thoughts. He believed "the ethers" were much quieter then. He began a daily dialogue with this guiding thread.

Guided by and from "headquarters" within, Charles and Myrtle began one of the greatest heart/head healing ministries the world has ever known and called it Unity. They invested every waking hour in prayer and meditation, writing down their ideas while seeking guidance and direction on how to proceed, starting from within and then taking their guidance without.

In 1892, Charles and Myrtle summed up their commitment to the threads that now bound them in Unity by penning their Dedication and Covenant:

We, Charles Fillmore and Myrtle Fillmore, husband and wife, hereby dedicate ourselves, our time, our money, all we have and all we expect to have, to the Spirit of Truth, and through it, to the Society of Silent Unity.

It being understood and agreed that the said Spirit of Truth shall render unto us an equivalent for this dedication, in peace of mind, health of body, wisdom, understanding, love, life, and an abundant supply of all things necessary to meet every want without our making any of these things the object of our existence.

In the presence of the Conscious Mind of Christ Jesus, this 7th day of December A.D. 1892.

Charles Fillmore
Myrtle Fillmore

Their willingness to pursue spiritual work echoes these words from Isaiah 6:8: "Then I heard the voice of the Lord saying, 'Whom shall I send, and who will go for us?' And I said, 'Here am I, Lord; send me!'" The hymn "Here I Am, Lord" is beloved especially by ministerial students seeking ordination in Unity.

'I Do Not Inherit Sickness'

In my own quest to find these unifying threads, my question has always been: How far back do these threads go? Perhaps they have always been there for humanity to uncover, discover, and begin weaving into our open hearts, minds, and ultimately bodies. We know they were certainly present to the cave dwellers of Australia with their concentric circles. We know with great certainty they were present in the life and ministry of Jesus more than 2,000 years ago as he touched so many minds and hearts. And now we know they were present in the 1800s with Myrtle and Charles Fillmore.

Today I am convinced that from the one unifying thread came the two (heart and mind), and there has emerged within me this amazing, infinite field of unlimited possibilities. This one thread, now expressing itself as twin threads (healing and guiding), make up the soul of every human—the thread of heart and the thread of mind. As I write this book, I now know that these threads have always been there for me and for you. They are waiting to find their way into the fabric of our lives at any level. If we look for it, we can discover in ourselves our very own access to these threads, which are available to any open heart and mind. These two unifying threads are forever woven into the fabric of your life and mine

Discovering this can bring new life to our bodies, new possibilities in all the other areas of our lives, and new connections that may unlock the mysteries of why we are here and what we are destined to become. Have you ever looked for your threads? Take a moment right now to meditate on these questions. Could it be that in your own life, there is a larger and more powerful tapestry waiting to emerge in you? And could that tapestry be the one that can lead you to find your own healing pathway? These are the questions that Donna and I have been asking ourselves.

The Fillmores' story has always inspired and intrigued us. We began to discover very early in our marriage that our connections to the Unity movement and to the path of healing came from the very same unifying thread and entered our lives through the pathways of heart and mind. As we began to weave our way through our roots, our history, and the amazing ways we have arrived at the place where we are, we discovered that these threads are even stronger today than we ever thought possible.

In the pages ahead, I will share more about Donna's and my own death sentences and our subsequent recoveries from cancer. We will also share how these unifying threads brought us together and continue to guide us in our adventures here on planet Earth. Suffice it to say, the quest for answers led both of us on an astonishing journey—not only a healing journey but one with so many other synchronicities.

This, then, has become the inspiration, the encouragement, and the blueprint not only for my healing but, as we shall see, for Donna's healing as she joined me in knowing that, as children of God, we are joint heirs to wholeness, wellness, and renewal. It means there's no room for sickness to remain in our experience.

Healing Is Our Destiny

What was it that guided Myrtle and Charles Fillmore to that lecture in Kansas City in 1886 to hear the very words that would bring personal healing, then guided them to start a prayer ministry in their home and join in prayer with others? What guided them to expand this into what would become a worldwide teaching called Unity, which would have as its center the practical application of spiritual principle? What guided Charles to wake at 2 a.m. each morning to "go to headquarters" to find the answers he was seeking?

I dare to believe these are the same threads that have guided me to write this book.

It all starts with a willingness to be open and receptive to a universe of infinite possibilities within us, which, we will soon discover, always has our back.

We all begin with one of these two truths. If healing is what is needed, we can start as Myrtle Fillmore did, knowing *I am a child of God, and therefore I do not inherit sickness.* Or if it's guidance we seek, wanting to connect with "headquarters," we can start as Charles Fillmore started, from a place where we know: *Here am I, Headquarters. Use me.*

If these two unifying principles were true for the Fillmores and are true for Donna and me, then they must be true for everyone, including you. It is our prayer that you will find and follow them on your healing journey to your Source.

No longer is healing an accidental, incidental happenstance or a legend. Healing is not something that happens to the lucky or a privileged few who can afford it. It is, in fact, our destiny. And more important, it's a practical, usable, doable process, available to anyone and everyone who is willing to put themselves directly in contact with their own personal, individual relationship with one or both of the unifying threads.

So with that as our rallying cry, we set sail on a journey that started we know not how long ago, when the tiny thread of hope was born and led to the absolute certainty of our healing and so much more!

Threads for Discussion ————————————————————————————

1. How can you make sure your own threads unfurl? Do you have any say in this?

2. Do you believe that everything in your life is predestined or accidental?

3. Do you believe in God? If yes, what is your current name for God? If not, why not?

Part One

THE HEALING THREAD

A HAIRCUT AND SO MUCH MORE!

Chapter 1

*I realized in all of the cases where I was happy
with the decision I made, there were two common
threads: Surround myself with the smartest people
who challenge you to think about things in new
ways and do something you are not ready to do so
you can learn the most.* —Marissa Mayer

Some years ago, a reporter asked the comedian Flip Wilson about his faith commitment.

"Oh, haven't you heard?" said Flip. "I'm a Jehovah's Bystander."

"A Jehovah's Bystander?" the reporter questioned. "I've never heard of a Jehovah's Bystander. What in the world is that?"

To which Flip Wilson replied, "Well, they asked me to be a witness, but I didn't want to get involved!"

Sometimes I have felt like a bystander on the sidelines of life, as though what was happening to me gave me no choice but to accept whatever was coming down the pike. At other times, I must admit, all I have really wanted was to be a bystander. We can watch things come and go in the lives of others, as well as what is happening in our own lives. We can be a spectator of the trials and tribulations that are taking place all around us and within us. We can stand on the sidelines of life feeling concern and compassion for those who are going through times of change and challenge, but we certainly don't really want any of that to happen to us. We are committed to safety and distance and trying to keep trouble and tribulation at arm's length, away from where we are living our small, private lives.

But you and I both know that's not how life works. Eventually we are pulled kicking and screaming into the fray until we find ourselves smack-dab in the middle of things over which we seem to have no control—things that hurt and challenge us, and some things that can do us in.

If we are to be *in* this world, we must, for a while, also be *of* this world. If we are in a human body, we will encounter some of the changes and challenges that every body endures.

In those moments, we can no longer stand by and be uninvolved in what is happening. Our body wants our immediate and complete attention, and it will have its way. If only we knew that what the body is calling for is the healing thread. The body is calling for something only your inner relationship to this thread can provide. But alas, the body dutifully follows any thread offered it.

Later in this book I will share a pattern of behavior that, most certainly, led me down a dim and dark hallway. Here's how things began to unravel for me.

On what seemed a ho-hum-nothing-special kind of day in August 2013, I left home to drive to what had become my favorite hair salon, for my favorite haircut, with my favorite hairstylist, Amanda.

Once seated in her chair, we embarked on our usual chats about this and that. After she had finished cutting my hair, she took out her electric shaver to give the usual trim to my neck. At that moment something weird happened.

As she was trimming my neck, suddenly she stopped and turned off the razor. She had been in the middle of one of her always-interesting stories but in mid-sentence, she said nothing. For what seemed like an exceptionally long and uncomfortable time, she was silent. This was not like her. She usually talked nonstop from first snip to last trim.

Finally, she came around from behind and stood in front of me. She had a puzzled look on her face and, looking deep into my eyes with a look I'd never seen before, she said, "David, what are those weird-looking lumps on the back of your neck?"

Seeking to downplay her discovery, which I didn't think was that obvious or that important, I replied that I did have some itching going on back there but hadn't really paid much attention to it. I smirked, hoping she would finish up soon, leave me alone, and send me on my way.

After a long, deep breath, she said, "*David*, you need to have those lumps looked at. They may be nothing, but they could be something!"

"Something like what?" I asked.

"I don't know. I'm only a hairstylist, but I've seen lumps like that before. And some of them have turned out to be quite serious."

I politely thanked her for her candid observation and advice, saying I would certainly have the lumps examined. I stood up and followed her to the cash register. We set an appointment six weeks ahead for my next haircut. I thanked her, tipped her, and we said our goodbyes.

As I was reaching for the door to leave, she called out, "Now, don't ignore those lumps, David! You have someone take a good, long look at them. And soon! Promise?"

I promised I would and went on my way.

One does not usually spend a whole lot of time thinking about what's going on in the back of one's neck. And so, I didn't think much about it until some days later when Donna blurted out these words: "What are those strange-looking lumps on the back of your neck? I've been noticing them for days now, and they're getting bigger and redder!"

She implored me to see my primary physician as soon as possible for a checkup.

In a few days, I was sitting in my doctor's office, and she was taking a long, medical look at the lumps—first with the naked eye, then with an eyeglass instrument. For what seemed like forever, she said nothing. Finally, she said, "David, I am not liking what I'm seeing back there. I am ordering an ultrasound for you."

Hmmm, I thought. An ultrasound! Never had one of those before.

Three days later I was lying on a long table with the buzz of an ultrasound machine droning in my ear. A technician was waving an interesting-looking wand over the back of my neck.

Hmm, I thought. Probably some sort of big pimple, or a spider bite, or maybe a tick or some sort of welt. Nothing more serious than that!

What I learned was that the body does not mess around. When it wants your complete and undivided attention—when it wants you to become more than a mere bystander in the story of your life—it will step in and send you clear and powerful signals. It will bring you face-to-face with who and what you thought you were, who and what you think you are, and who and what you are to become.

Threads for Discussion

1. What was an experience you had where your body got your complete and absolute attention? Is there something that happened in your life that you first thought was no big thing, but you found out later was a *really, really big thing?*

2. How did you respond? Did you shrug it off? Or act?

3. If you shrugged it off, what was the result?

4. If you acted, what was the result?

5. What did you learn about yourself through this experience?

THE DIN OF A DIRE DIAGNOSIS
Chapter 2

A spider lives inside my head who weaves a
strange and wondrous web of silken threads and
silver strings to catch all sorts of flying things, like
crumbs of thoughts and bits of smiles and specks of
dried-up tears, and dust of dreams that catch and
cling for years and years and years ...
—Shel Silverstein

One of my all-time favorite rock 'n' roll bands growing up was Dire Straits. They had many great hits, but the one I loved the most (in fact, it is the ringer on my cell phone) is called "Walk of Life."

Along the road of life that you and I walk, there are moments we might consider *dire*. Among other things, the word means "great fear or suffering, dreadful, terrible circumstances, misfortune, disaster, and desperation."

I am happy to report that my walk of life up to this point had been relatively "dire free." Other than the sad and sudden departure of my first wife, there was nothing I would put in the dire category. *Dire*, to my way of thinking, is the end of the road and most certainly the end of all hope. But here I was about to enter a door marked *Dire* as never before. I was to come face to face with my own swift and sure demise from planet Earth.

My doctor came directly to the point. "David, you have cancer. Probably melanoma, but I don't know for sure. I'm sending you to a cancer specialist. He will take a sample and send it to a laboratory for detailed analysis. I trust it's nothing too serious, but it needs your *immediate* attention."

Within 48 hours, I found myself in the office of a cancer surgeon, who performed a biopsy on my now nearly shaven neck. He told me to return in three days and he would have a report.

The day of the report came all too soon. As Donna and I sat in his office, he didn't wait on formalities as he came charging in with the report in hand and a student following him, saying, "McClure, take your clothes off!"

I was about to hear news I never dreamed I would hear. "You've got Stage 4 metastatic melanoma and I want to see where it started on your skin."

I looked at Donna, who was already weeping, and asked my life partner, who is also a hospital chaplain, "What does *metastatic* mean?"

She told me it meant the cancer had already spread to other parts of my body. It wasn't just in those lumps, but probably also in my lymph nodes and perhaps beyond that.

The specialist concurred.

Up to that point, I didn't know what being run over by a cement truck felt like, but I think I do now. What does he mean by *Stage 4 metastatic melanoma*? He can't be talking about me! Not the Very Reverend David W. McClure! Not the son of my dear mom and dad! Not the happy-go-lucky guy who loved to laugh, joke, kibitz, and play in the sun. (Ah, "play in the sun"—more about that later.) And certainly not the almost clean-living, clean-eating, never-smoking, one-glass-of-wine-a-month, always-brushing-my-teeth, sometimes-going-to-the-gym kind of guy I had been for more than 70 years. Not him! Not *moi!*

Not since I had discovered that my first wife had left me for good and was never coming home again had I felt so sucker punched. There was nothing in my memory banks that could approach this pronouncement in any shape or form. There was no file drawer in my mind or anywhere in the halls of my consciousness where what I had just heard had ever been recorded. What this good doctor and bearer of dire tidings was telling me was such an affront to my very being, my self-image, my future on planet Earth, that I could hardly comprehend its significance and impact. As Donna and I walked out of the doctor's office (at least, I think we walked out, although I'm not sure of that), we were both numbed to the core.

When I returned home, I googled The Skin Cancer Foundation and discovered, "More than two people every hour die of skin cancer." That's all I needed to know. No more googling on this subject for me! Nothing could have prepared us for such a dire, dismal diagnosis. Was this the end of the line, the end of my rope for this incarnation?

I learned that just when you think things cannot get any worse, they can and sometimes do. But at the same time, just when you think you have no more inner strength, trust, faith, and gumption, you do. Just when you think you have heard the worst or the best, you haven't.

So, here I am, I thought. I'm 76 years old. I've had a good run at life. I've traveled all over the planet. I have the best wife in the world. I've served in some pretty spectacular ministries including Hawaii two times, Vancouver, Australia, and Dallas, plus others, over the past 60 years. I even got to speak in Carnegie Hall. I've written articles for Unity publications. I had a great childhood with amazing parents. My brothers and sister were always loving and supportive. When I actually think about it, I've had an amazing life.

Perhaps it's my time to mosey on down the road and be grateful for what I've had.

But perhaps not.

I still haven't written that book I've been saying I will write one day. There are a few items on my bucket list—more places I'd like to see and adventures I'd like for Donna and me to discover.

After mulling all of this in my mind, I turned to the guiding thread within me. *Here I am, Lord, use me!* Or lose me? The answer came in an instant. *Go and have the surgery.* The road ahead might have some potholes and some rough spots, but I decided if I could squeeze a few more months out of life, that would be fine and dandy with me.

Threads for Discussion

1. When was your time of deepest, direst despair? What happened?

2. Was this the lowest point in your life? How did it feel and how did you manage it?

3. What form did your despair take?

4. If you are reading this, you obviously survived the worst that life has thrown your way. What tools, methods, or ideas did you use to find your way through it?

5. How did you go about it?

BEYOND DESPAIR

Chapter 3

*May a thread of comfort be woven through your
difficult days.* —Mary Anne Radmacher

I made a promise when I started to write this book that I would
inject some humor into my storyline. After telling you of my
visit to what I can now call the "lump dump," I believe a touch
of something funny is called for. So here's a popular story I have
used in a sermon or two:

Sitting by the window of her convent, Sister Barbara opened a
letter from home one evening. Inside the letter was a $100 bill her
parents had sent. She smiled at the gesture. As she read the letter
by the window's light, she looked out and noticed a shabbily
dressed stranger leaning against the lamppost below.

Quickly, she wrote "Don't despair—Sister Barbara" on a piece
of paper, wrapped it in the $100 bill, and when she knew she had
the man's attention, she tossed it out the window to him.

The stranger picked it up and, with a somewhat puzzled
expression and the tip of his hat, went off down the street.

The next day, Sister Barbara was told that a man was at the
door, insisting on seeing her. She went down and found the
stranger waiting. Without a word, he handed her a huge wad of
$100 bills.

"What's this?" she asked.

"That's the $8,000 you have coming, Sister," he replied. "*Don't
Despair* paid 80-to-1!"

Like the man in that story, I could have bet on that horse, but
instead I seemed to be headed deeper into despair no matter what
the odds. It felt as though I had been pushed to the edge of a cliff
and was about to be pushed all the way over.

I was referred to a surgeon who had been selected for me,
whose task was to remove the lumps from my neck, plus whatever
else he could find back there, or down there, that was considered
troubling. If you think the cancer specialist's news was dire, wait
until you hear the news this chap was about to give me.

Sitting in his office, among the first words out of his mouth were these: "David, I hate to tell you this, but what you've got is the worst diagnosis a human being can possibly have. Hardly anyone lives more than a few months with what you've got."

Mmm, boy! Thank you for sharing, Doc!

And so began my encounter with the doctor I came to call "Mack the Knife." What a way to start a relationship! I didn't think I was going to like this young surgeon but later I came to praise and appreciate this guy for saving my life. But not right then! Not just yet! I was still despairing.

From where I sat he might as well have handed me my obituary in a handbasket. My thoughts turned to Mother Myrtle's terminal TB diagnosis. All I thought that was left for him to say was: "Been nice knowin' ya! See ya later, alligator."

He went on to say that Stage 4 melanoma is the deadliest of all skin cancers. It was Stage 4 gone wild, meaning it was metastatic. Cancer was rapidly spreading to other parts of my body.

He looked me in the eye and laid it on the line: "I'm sorry to inform you that you only have a few months to live, if that. I'm going to operate on you and will do the best that I can, but all it's going to do is extend your life by a little."

Hoping he might be able to give me some months beyond a "few," I asked him, "What kind of operation is it?"

He said (are you ready for this?), "It's called a modified radical dissection."

Now isn't that special? I could feel every cell in my body shake and shudder. What I didn't know was that I was about to lose not only all the cancerous tissue in my neck but a whole bunch of lymph nodes in that vicinity.

My pal, "Mack" the surgeon, reminded me that, because my melanoma was metastatic, he could do nothing about any other internal organs in my body where the Big C might be lurking and already working.

And so, with a heart that was slowly sinking slightly lower than my knees—where cancer might already be making itself at home—I offered a feeble blessing to my faithful and lifelong (so far) companion—my neck—and dragged myself out of Mack's office and into the hospital for some rad knife cutting.

Apparently, the operation went well. Thanks to the anesthesiologist, I didn't notice any undue pain or discomfort, save the fact that *Despair* was still gaining ground on *Don't Despair* in the race to save my life.

Later I learned that the melanoma had indeed spread to other parts of my body and that, yes, my days on planet Earth, from a medical point of view, were officially numbered.

Have you ever been picked on when you were down? My older brothers used to hold me down and tickle me, or breathe peanut butter breath into my face, or rub supper leftovers in my face. But *this* was true torture. This was what I imagine waterboarding might be like.

I felt totally helpless and totally—more than a mile—beyond despair. What I learned is, even when all the forces of the world are stacked against you and impending doom seems like the only course of action, you still have resources within you to draw from. You're still kickin'!

Threads for Discussion ————————————————————

1. Have you ever received news, either about your body, your relationship, or your finances that seemed like "the end of the road" or "the end of the world" for you? What was that news?

2. How did you feel about that?

3. What did you do about it?

4. Did you run out of resources, faith, or ideas? Or did you find an inner strength?

5. Do you think there is a spiritual way to keep medical issues from happening?

6. If something medical happens to you, does it have to do with your consciousness?

SAY AMEN WITH AMENDS

Chapter 4

Sometimes you only get one chance to rewrite the qualities of the character you played in a person's life story. Always take it. Never let the world read the wrong version of you.—Shannon L. Alder

As I was thinking about this chapter, I started wondering what the difference was between the word amen and the word amend. Is there a thread there?

Looking it up in my trusty *Funk & Wagnalls*, I learned that amen comes at the end of something—a prayer, a chapter, or a life. *Amend*, on the other hand, means to make better.

Thinking that I might be coming to the amen place in my life due to my diagnosis, I felt guided to see whether I could try to set things right and make amends with the people I might have hurt, harmed, or handcuffed over the years.

It was then that I remembered something I had read a while back, going through several of my old books and files. It was in a pamphlet titled "How I Found Health," written by Unity cofounder Myrtle Fillmore, reproduced from the article first published in *Unity Magazine* in 1897.

She wrote: "I asked my body for forgiveness for the foolish, ignorant course that I had pursued in the past, when I had condemned it and called it weak, inefficient, and diseased."

Having had my melanoma surgery, I sat down to begin the process of making peace with the rest of my past and getting my affairs in order. If what Mack the Knife said was right and I only had a few months left on earth, I'd better tie up as many loose ends as possible.

Okay, David, where do you begin? Oh, yes, how will Donna be provided for? Is my life insurance up to date? Have I paid all my bills? Did I take those books back to the library? Is my underwear clean?

Unaccustomed as I was to dying (at least, I don't remember the death part in my other lives), I wasn't sure where to start. I would think of one thing and then 10 more things would suddenly occur to me, which seemed even more important than what was important an hour ago.

I had informed my family of my impending demise—check. Close friends came next, followed by my Facebook friends. Where should I start with amends? I guessed I would just plunge in, so I did.

One thing that kept entering my mind was that I wanted to leave the planet with a sense that I had made things as right as I could with those I would leave behind. I'd always liked Jesus' words: "So when you are offering your gift at the altar, if you remember that your brother or sister has something against you, leave your gift there before the altar and go; first be reconciled to your brother or sister, and then come and offer your gift" (Matthew 5:23-24).

To me, "reconciled" meant making amends. Forgiving and asking to be forgiven.

I started making a list of those I felt had something against me or with whom I might have something still pending. I wanted to leave my slate and my plate as clean as possible before making my imminent departure from this "mortal coil."

As I was thinking of all the people I knew and have known throughout my life, it also occurred to me that I needed to say goodbye to my very own, amazing body, which had served me well for more than 70 years at that time. I thought I would start this amending/forgiving process as Mother Myrtle had—with my nearest neighbor, my very own body temple.

This body of mine was currently responding in a manner that suggested I had done something to contribute to the symptoms that were currently showing up inside of it. Was it something I ate or did not eat? Was it not exercising enough or, as I suspected, perhaps it was subjecting my body to hours upon hours of lying in the sun, getting a bronze body to impress all the girls and my less-than-satisfied ego?

I thought back to those prolonged adventures with my friend, the sun. From the get-go I had languished in the rays. I had lived in places where the sun was the star attraction—Hawaii and Australia. I had spent hours as a boy trying to get a tan, lying prone on the dock at Port Sydney, Ontario. Good grief, I was born halfway between the North Pole and the equator! There were plenty of minutes, days, and hours in the sun that had slowly taken their toll on my tender, white, Canadian body.

I googled The Skin Cancer Foundation again and found this glorious statistic: "On average, a person's risk for melanoma doubles if they have had more than five sunburns, but just one blistering sunburn in childhood or adolescence more than doubles a person's chances of developing melanoma later in life." So better late than never, here was a great place to say amen to too much sun, curtail my exposure, and forgive myself for my past indiscretions with our nearest star.

To make amends to my body, I started with the most obvious area—the back of my neck—but then realized the melanoma was metastatic and had spread to lymph nodes, organs, and bones. I blessed every square inch of my anatomy and thanked it for its years of service on my behalf. I thanked it for the privilege of living a healthy life and having the strength and vitality to do and be many, many things.

Having given my body a major vote of thanks and apologizing for too much time in the sun, too much ice cream, and too many days sitting in my La-Z-Boy when I should have been out jogging or playing pickleball, my mind turned to other humans I might have mistreated, ignored, or misjudged. Then there were the people I might have perceived as mistreating or misjudging me. I wanted to clear the air with everything and everyone who came to mind. I jotted down a list of those I thought had wronged me, those I had wronged, and anyone with unfinished business still on my books.

At the top of the list was my first wife, who after about 12 years of marriage decided not to come home one night in 1977 and took off to begin a new life with another guy. And what about the guy? Surely, as much as I resisted the idea, I needed to forgive him too.

And so began a major, wholesale housecleaning of my mind and memory banks, plus all the corners of my cluttered consciousness.

First out of the starting gate was a long email to my ex-wife, as well as one to her now-husband who had "stolen" her away in the night decades ago. Then there was a small list of other folks, living in various parts of the world, who got communications from me designed to clear the air and make sure I was okay in their books as they were in mine.

I dug as deeply as I could into the past, even going back to some of my childhood friends. One example is a kid named Billy who had lived down the street from me. I had "under-counted" the number of comic books I had borrowed from him and never returned. I even wanted to make that right. We used to trade not only comic books but trading cards, marbles, and agates.

To my surprise, I received warm and encouraging responses from these folks, thanking me for making amends and for releasing them from all blame, hurt, and humiliation I might have carried with me over the years. And they, in turn, set me free from a list of grievances I never even realized *they* were keeping track of—some for a long, long time.

And, dear reader, if you are someone I may have hurt, embarrassed, or snubbed somewhere along the path, I want to offer to you, right here and right now, my humblest apology.

Having sent off messages of amends to anyone and everyone who had "aught against me," there remained one last soul on my list. And that was the dear, sweet soul who said *yes* to my popped question nearly 30 years before: Donna.

Surely neither of us was holding on to any stuff. Surely!

An opportunity for us to clear the air came after we had been invited to spend a week at our friends' log home at Priest Lake, Idaho. Our friends were going to be away, so we had this idyllic hideaway to ourselves, a perfect setting to iron out whatever issues might still be unresolved between us.

After enjoying our inspiring surroundings, taking a long walk on the beach and in the woods, and enjoying a delicious meal, it was then time to face the music and deal with the issues at hand.

We took turns bringing up issues we believed were still standing in the way of an already amazing relationship. Even in the lives of a happily married couple, there are issues—some harder to talk about than others—that can still be resolved, negotiated, and forgiven.

We were both amazed at what the other party brought up to be addressed. But with each expression of forgiveness and amends, we felt a new lightness of being coming over us. It was a remarkable weekend that we shall never forget.

I felt that finally I could say amen to my amends. With my affairs now somewhat in a state of orderly order, it was time to move on to what was next.

I want to share with you what I learned from this purifying, cleansing, healing amendment to my life. When Jesus was on the cross, he was apparently overheard saying, "Forgive them, Father; for they know not what they are doing" (Luke 23:34). For me, the key part of that sentence was "know not." If there is a "sin" that you and I commit in life, it is because we know not. Our only "sin" is our ignorance of the Truth that we are—every one of us—a beautiful, radiant child of the one presence and the one power—the unifying thread. When we lose sight of who and what we really are, we do stuff to one another, we say stuff, we forget stuff. And that's when stuff happens.

Again, from Jesus: "You will know the truth and the truth will set you free" (John 8:32).

Threads for Discussion ————————————————

1. What are some situations in which you have received forgiveness from another person? Was it a surprise to you? Did you welcome that forgiveness into your life? And what was the ultimate outcome?

2. What are some situations in which you have forgiven another person? Was it a surprise to the other person? What was the result?

3. Is there someone right now that you have yet to forgive? Would you be willing to make amends with this person now? If so, please put this in motion. If not, why not?

4. Did you ever blame yourself or someone else for what is happening to you?

AS THE PAGE TURNS

Chapter 5

*I will repay you for the years that the swarming
locust has eaten.* —Joel 2:25

It was one thing to forgive my body. But what more was asked of
me before I said goodbye to it? My body is my nearest neighbor,
after all, and Jesus told us to love our neighbor as ourselves. So
I knew it was time for me to have a "come to Jesus" talk with my
body. This dear body of mine had served me well over the decades
and, up until the cancer thing, I had few complaints. And my
body, for the most part, had reciprocated with what I considered
above-average health.

Once again, looking for inspiration and direction from the
many books on my bookshelf, I turned to the ancient but truly
relevant words of Mother Myrtle in her priceless pamphlet, "How
I Found Health."

Growing up in Unity from the age of 7, I had heard the
story of Myrtle's fabled healing a hundred times before. I had
given sermons around her healing a few times. Now here I was,
returning to her written words in my time of need. Her story
is one that has amazed and astounded thousands of people all
over the world. I was preparing to be amazed and astounded one
more time. I found myself rereading and rediscovering how her
healing took place and what steps she had taken to add more than
40 years to her life after doctors had given her only months to
live. In turning her pages, I felt I, too, could move toward my own
healing. There were still things on my bucket list that I wanted to
complete, including writing a book. I had sermons to give, places
to travel, but above all, I wanted more years with my dear Donna.

Mother Myrtle's story mentioned that her turnaround began
almost immediately after she heard Dr. E.B. Weeks say those
astonishing words: *I am a child of God, and therefore I do not
inherit sickness.* Accepting for most of her life that she had
inherited her ill health and limited circumstances from her
parents and ancestors, Myrtle found Weeks' bold declaration to

be an astonishing pronouncement. The story goes that she wrote the statement down and placed it on her mirror at home where she could refer to it and affirm it many times a day.

Reading further in her book, *How to Let God Help You*, where the same essay appears, I saw that this was only the beginning of her healing journey. What came next was even more soul-opening for me. She wrote:

> I have made what seems to me a discovery. I was very sick; I had all the ills of mind and body that I could bear. Medicine and doctors ceased to give me relief and I was in despair, until I found practical Christianity.
>
> I affirmed my beliefs, and I was healed. I did most of the healing myself because I wanted the understanding for future use. This is how I made what I call my discovery:
>
> Life has to be guided by intelligence in making all forms. The same law works in my own body. Life is simply a form of energy, and it has to be guided and directed in a person's body by his or her intelligence. How do we communicate intelligence? By thinking and talking, of course. Then it flashed upon me that I might talk to the life in every part of my body and have it do just what I wanted. I began to teach my body and got marvelous results.
>
> I told the life in my liver that it was not torpid or inert, but full of vigor and energy. I told the life in my stomach that it was not weak or inefficient, but energetic, strong, and intelligent. I told the life in my abdomen that it was no longer infested with ignorant ideas of disease, put there by myself and by doctors, but that it was all alive with the sweet, pure, wholesome energy of God. I told my limbs that they were active and strong. I told my eyes that they did not see of themselves, but that they

expressed the sight of Spirit and that they were drawing on an unlimited source. I told them that they were young eyes—clear, bright eyes, because the light of God shone through them.

I told my heart that the pure love of Jesus Christ flowed in and through its beatings and that all the world felt its joyous pulsation. I went to all the life centers in my body and spoke words of Truth to them—words of strength and power ...

I told them that they were no longer in bondage to the carnal mind; that they were not corruptible flesh, but centers of life and energy omnipresent.

Wow! I embraced each and every one of these words as though I were reading them for the first time. Was this a key element to a healing formula that not only worked for Myrtle but that I or anyone else could take to heart, practice, and find miraculous results with?

There and then, I began an extended series of conversations not only with the organs, bones, and tissues that had been impacted by the cancer but to every corner and cranny in this thing I called my physical body, now with a certain confidence that all its parts were listening and, more important, responding.

I reminded my body of what I knew to be the Truth about me—that I was a spiritual being, living in a spiritual universe, and governed by spiritual laws. I remember centering on a nightly chat with my neck, kidneys, colon, lungs, and back.

I tried to get a few words into every part of my body, telling it that I loved it, that I recognized the healing resilience within it, and that the activity of the healing thread was already taking charge "in there" and "down there."

After spending a portion of every day and sometimes every night on this lovefest with my body, it occurred to me—if living flesh can respond to thought and the spoken word, what about inanimate objects like machines, medical instruments, knives, scalpels, test tubes, and so on? A wild and crazy notion? Perhaps. But why not?

I began to think about the many inanimate medical machines and instruments that I would be encountering in the days ahead.

My medical team, led by my oncologist at Cancer Care Northwest in Spokane, Washington, had told me that, while they did not hold out much hope for any dramatic results, they were going to throw a Hail Mary pass and see if they could somehow turn things around for me and perhaps add a few more months to my life.

Having surgically and successfully removed the most obvious signs of melanoma—the lumps in my neck, including 75 lymph nodes in the surrounding area—the next course of action was a full round of radiation. A full round was six weeks, three times a week.

I remember quite clearly walking into the radiation room for my first treatment. Two smiling female technicians warmly greeted me. After smiling a tentative smile, my attention quickly turned to the large, tube-shaped machine at the end of the small room I had just entered. There it was.

As I suspected, this was the radiation unit that would be my roasting/toasting companion for this stage of my treatment. The technicians informed me that, before I could start the zapping, I would first have to undergo the business of fitting me with a mask to wear over my head, neck, and chest to protect me from the "death ray" at the other end of the room.

Once the mask was made and fitted to my exact specifications, I decided this was a good time to try out my new "talking to stuff" theory. Yes, I was going to talk directly to this thing that was now ready to be placed over my face.

One last look in the mirror showed me this mask resembled either a fencing shield or a mask for hockey goalies. Growing up in Canada, I knew the mask was an essential part of the goalie's hockey equipment. I named this gizmo Turk Broda after an outstanding net-minder who played for the Toronto Maple Leafs during my childhood years.

Okay, so far, so good. Me and Turk, the mask, were now on a first-name basis. And while the technicians were not looking or hearing, I began to talk to Turk. I told him that he had tremendous goal-tending skills. I told him that he had the power to keep out all harmful rays, letting in nothing but healing energy. And from that day forward, each time I went into the machine, I made sure to praise and give thanks for Turk.

The radiation device was another matter. The brand name for it was Elekta. I had done a little reading up on her before going near for my first treatment. She (I decided that it was going to be a *she* for me) was a state-of-the-art, image-guided, radiation therapy system that was said to be loaded with a set of comprehensive treatment solutions to give patients the best treatment possible. Yeah, sure.

As I entered the radiation room for my first full-fledged treatment, I took one more glance at this big hummer as she sat at the end of this small chamber. I say *hummer* because they already had her warming up, and she made a distinct humming sound.

The two always-smiling, always-positive technicians greeted me once again. Only this time, they added the words "Welcome aboard" as they gently guided me onto the loading tray. After fitting me with Turk, it was suddenly goodbye to hockey night in Canada. I began to feel more like Hannibal Lecter in the movie, *The Silence of the Lambs*, waiting for my "fava beans and a nice Chianti."

Up until now, I had not been prone to much claustrophobia. I had had my share of MRIs over the years, but as they strapped me down and slid me into range of the menacing and watchful eye of the radiation gun, I felt the world closing in around me.

My first thoughts were, *Here I am, inside Turk, and now trapped inside something I have never encountered before.* All sorts of scary and menacing thoughts and feelings began to bombard me from all sides.

Quickly, I searched for something to hold onto. And then I remembered my vow to talk to things.

I started with Turk. I told him he was my goalie. He knew how to keep bad stuff from happening to me. He knew how to let only good stuff in. It took a few minutes during that first session to relax a little as I found and hung onto my inner goalie.

But what about this now humming, chirping, hissing radiation machine? As I listened and peeked out from the tiny holes in Turk the Mask, the Elekta began to take a stroll around my head, stopping from time to time, finding its target, I guess, and then moving on to another part of my neck. Occasionally it seemed to me that it was amping up its horsepower then zapping me with whatever Elekta machines shoot at you.

I struggled to think of a name to call her. Suddenly, a name came through as clear as a bell: *Radiance.* I would henceforth call this hummer Radiance!

At the very moment her name popped into my head, I relaxed. I'm sure my pulse and blood pressure went down measurably. *Ahh,* I said to myself. *Here is another member of my healing team. Radiance is now cheering for me and not against me. Now she's on my side. She will not nor can she hurt me. She can give me a tan and turn my skin into toast, but I feel there's going to be a positive end to all of this.*

And toast well done it was! After six weeks of talking to machines and the occasional technician, I looked as if I had spent a whole vacation on Lanikai, my favorite beach in Hawaii.

I *wished* that I were on Lanikai but then reflected on the fact that Donna and I had lived in Hawaii for a total of 15 years, ministering both in Honolulu and Kailua. And one thing they had a whole lot of over there was sun! And one thing we loved to do was lie in the sun and get a tan. That was probably where melanoma became my traveling companion.

I wondered whether my talking to machines and stuff would have any effect on my situation. I certainly hoped and prayed this might turn the page.

What I learned from this process of transforming inanimate objects into friendlier, healing instruments, I began to apply, knowing that I was not the first person on earth to do this. In fact,

Jesus did it several times. He blessed the water and it became wine. He blessed bread and fish and turned them into enough to feed multitudes. He turned the cross on which he was to be crucified into a plus sign. The stone they placed in front of his tomb suddenly rolled away. How this could have happened, we do not know. But somebody gave that stone a good talking to!

Threads for Discussion ————————————————————

1. Have you ever talked to your body? Did you bless it or curse it? What was the result you experienced?

2. Have you ever forgiven your body for any pain or discomfort it has brought to you? What was the result of that experience?

3. Have you ever thanked your body for the pleasure and well-being it has given you? What was the result of that experience?

4. Have you ever talked to a machine or inanimate object? What was the nature of your conversation and what results, if any, did you witness?

BUT WAIT! A GAME CHANGER!
Chapter 6

When we try to pick out anything by itself, we find
it hitched to everything else in the universe.
—John Muir

By this time in my treatment program, I was looking everywhere in my life for as much cheering up as I could find. I remembered that, at least twice in the Bible, Jesus told folks to cheer up and not to be such gloomy grouches.

On one occasion Jesus was trying to cheer on Peter to walk on water. Peter, encouraged by his teacher, got out of the boat and started to walk on the water toward Jesus, who was already wading through the waves. Peter was doing all right until he turned his attention toward the wind and waves and the fact that he was *really walking on water!* Immediately he began to sink.

The other time Jesus tried to cheer us on was when he said something to the effect that if your attention is on what's going on in the world—or, I think I could add, what's happening in your body—you will have what he called *tribulation,* which means Trouble with a capital T. So Jesus our Way Shower and teacher told us, "Be of good cheer!" (John 16:33 KJV) The New Revised Standard Version is translated: "Take courage!" Either way, Jesus wanted us to get out of our gloom and doom and look for positives.

All of us can use a cheering section in our lives from time to time, especially when we start to tribulate. At this stage, I was doing a lot of tribulating about my predicament.

One Sunday, after delivering what I felt was a lackluster sermon pouring out of a dying man, Donna and I didn't wait for our usual handshaking at the end of a sermon—a sermon that, to this day, I can't remember. We slipped out of the building and headed home for more of our favorite pastime at this point: moping and sulking and tribulating.

After a short period and quickly tiring of MS&T, I decided to distract myself and turn on the TV to watch some football. My favorite team is the Seattle Seahawks. On this day, they were playing the Tennessee Titans. If you think I was down and depressed *before* coming home, the way this game was going was sending me deeper into the doldrums.

The Titans stepped out to a commanding lead and halfway through the fourth quarter, I found myself about as far down in my La-Z-Boy as I could possibly get. I was about to turn the TV off, when a sound—clear, bold, and loud—began to roar out of my TV speakers. This was not an unfamiliar sound to me. I had heard it many times before. It was a sound that had always inspired and uplifted me. But this time it was different. This time I heard a gazillion more decibels than I had ever heard before. I thought my eardrums would shatter.

The sound was that of the collective body of Seahawk fans— better known as the "12s"—cheering, yelling, screaming, and lifting the roof off the stadium.

It reminded me of Joshua leading his army to surround the city of Jericho and then encouraging them to shout as loudly as they possibly could. And, as we know, "the walls came a-tumbling down."

For those not familiar with football and the 12th man concept, it started with Texas A&M University. Each team is allowed only 11 players in the game at any one time. The Aggies of A&M believed they could create an extra player with the enthusiasm of their fans in the stands. They began to call the fans "the 12th man."

In 2006, the Aggies and the Seahawks made a deal allowing the Seahawks to also use the 12th man idea.

The number 12 is a great number for us clergy people. Twelve can be found in 187 places in the Bible—22 in Revelation alone. Jacob (Israel) had 12 sons, each of whom represented a tribe begun by a prince. Ishmael, who was born to Abraham through Hagar, also had 12 princes. God specified that 12 unleavened cakes of bread were to be placed every week in the temple. Jesus had 12 disciples—and the biblical 12s go on and on.

Metaphysically, Charles Fillmore suggested that 12 symbolizes wholeness and completion. He wrote in his ground-breaking book, *The Twelve Powers*, "The subconscious realm in man has 12 great centers of action, with 12 presiding egos or identities. When Jesus had attained a certain soul development, He called His twelve apostles to Him. This means that when man is developing out of mere personal consciousness into spiritual consciousness, he begins to train deeper and larger powers; he sends his thought down into the inner centers of his organism, and through his word quickens them to life."

And so, back to the game! That afternoon, the Seattle 12s broke the decibel record for an NFL stadium. It was louder than any roar that had ever been heard at any football game, college or professional. As the roar of the 12s reached a crescendo, I watched the whole tempo of the game shift. In that moment, the Hawks found their second wind.

One good play led to another and soon they were marching down the field, moving the ball, running over and around the Titans, and most important, scoring points. Followed by more points.

Finally, in the last seconds of the fourth quarter, the Seahawks got the go-ahead touchdown and won the game, thanks to their earsplitting hooting and hollering 12s. Talk about a cheering section!

I found myself standing up and cheering like one of the 12s. Donna, who was in the kitchen at the time, came in to see what all the noise was about. I told her about the 12s, and we both broke into a cheer of our own. It was the first time in a long time that I had had anything to cheer about.

This marked a game-changing turning point in my attitude about life and my situation. Sitting down for a football game that afternoon and hearing one of the loudest affirmations of life I had ever heard proved to be exactly what my inner doctor had ordered. I began to feel some of the "walls" that had held me in captivity to my illness beginning to crumble.

It triggered what was to be the most important spirit-lifter I had ever experienced. Immediately, I sat up straight in my chair, followed by jumping to my feet and standing up straighter and taller than I had for weeks. I began to believe in myself again. I might have thought all was lost when it really wasn't. There is something astounding, something certain, beyond where hope can take you.

I told Donna that if a football team could have a cheering section like that, then so could I. I would create my own 12th Man/Woman Healing Support Team!

I immediately started a list of those I wanted in my healing cheering section. I began with all those on my medical team—my primary care team, my oncologist and his team, my radiologist and his team, and yes, even Mack the Knife.

To this list, I added my family, my prayer partners at church, my Master Mind Prayer Group, Silent Unity (the prayer ministry of the global Unity movement started by Charles and Myrtle Fillmore long ago), folks from ministries I had previously served, Donna's colleagues at Sacred Heart Medical Center, even some folks whose stores I frequented, and last but certainly not least, approximately 5,000 Facebook friends and followers I had at the time.

In contacting them all, I confided in them about the death sentence I had initially been given by my medical staff. I told them about my Seahawks 12th Man experience. And then I asked them to join my 12th Person Healing Team and invited them to send me their prayerful and moral support if they felt so guided.

Within hours of sending out my SOS, I received dozens, then hundreds, of positive responses. What surprised me most was that, even with the dire diagnosis that was still staring me in the face, the majority of my newly formed 12s not only offered prayerful hope but also the certainty that the healing thread had my back and that healing was on its way!

Buoyed by this cheering section, I began to think of what my next moves would be on this astounding journey. What was before me on the road ahead? How different life can be for us when we have encouragement. What an uplifting experience it is when we know we are not alone in what we are confronting.

I think that was the main thing I got out of this experience. When you think you are all alone with your predicament, that's when you hear the roar of the crowd. You find you have this huge, amazing cheering section. There are hundreds, perhaps thousands, who can see beyond where you alone can see. They can believe beyond your unbelief. They can roar when you whimper. When you're backed up on the one-yard line, they can open a path to run for a touchdown.

Threads for Discussion ————————————————————————

1. Who have been the main cheerleaders in your life—those who have encouraged and supported you during trying times?

2. What is one situation you have gone through (or we can say "grown through") where you felt you were not alone?

3. Have you been a cheerleader in someone else's life? What were the circumstances?

4. How important would you say it is to have someone stand with you in times of challenge, or to stand with others during their predicament?

TREE HUGS: A TRIP TO MUIR WOODS

Chapter 7

Trees are so huge that they shut you up.
—Anne Lamott

I've always felt I had a decent cheering section in nature. I believed I was on speaking terms with many of the creatures and living things on planet Earth. Especially trees.

It was author Matthew Silverstone, who wrote the book *Blinded by Science*, who presented evidence that if you hang out with trees, you are sure to pick up tons of negative ions, which I've discovered are good for you. The Taoist viewpoint has always been that because trees are grounded in one place, they are able to transmute energy and absorb universal forces. One of the first poems I read in junior high was Joyce Kilmer's magnificent tribute to a tree.

In the process of forming my 12th Person Healing Team, I decided to take a step or two beyond a human healing team. I needed all the help I could get. So I decided to let trees share their energies and their healing vibes. Not just any trees, although I love them all. I wanted to call in some of the tallest and strongest trees I could find. That meant going to a spot that has always been for me and thousands of others a sacred and inspiring place—Muir Woods, just outside of San Francisco, California. There is a grove of giant redwoods there that I fell in love with when I was a minister in the City by the Bay. I had previously introduced Donna to "my redwoods," and she was the first one to suggest we pay them a visit once again.

It was around Thanksgiving 2014 that we arrived in San Rafael, California, which would be our home base while visiting our tree friends. The next morning, we took the short drive to the Muir Woods National Monument. We were surprised to find the parking lots already full of visitors. There are several public parking areas, but there were no open spots.

Dejected and discouraged, we were about to leave and try again the next day. But a voice inside told me to go back to the main parking area, the one nearest the entrance to the monument. Just as we drove in to look around, a car that was parked right next to the gate pulled out, and we pulled in. We could not have parked any closer to our tree friends! Once again, as Donna and I have done all our married lives, we took this as a sign that we were in the right place at the right time.

Entering the sanctuary of redwoods, one immediately feels the energy of these gentle giants. The air is cool and clean. As we walked among these old-growth coastal redwoods, cooling their roots in the fresh water of Redwood Creek and lifting their crowns to reach the sun and fog, we felt as though we were entering a church—truly the holy of holies.

These federally protected trees have been a national monument since 1908. This primeval forest is both refuge and laboratory, revealing to us and all who walk here a relationship with a living landscape. As we went deeper into the forest, we wondered what these giants might have to share with us today.

After giving my customary hug to a few of my old tree friends and waiting for direction and guidance—or perhaps, (dare I think this?) an instantaneous healing—we heard and felt nothing. Then I received my healing message—not from the trees but from Donna.

I decided to film a video of her at a special place in the middle of the grove. As I pointed my cell phone in her direction, she said, "Our spirit has been lifted. Our souls have been touched. And our bodies have been renewed. The atmosphere we are in right now is dense and full of life. Greenery, dirt, and water, hundreds of years old—even a thousand years old—it's almost like the very beginning of time itself, touching you and me in an amazing way! Can you feel that, David?"

I felt it. It was as though the very Voice of the Universe, talking through the trees and then through Donna, was announcing that these trees, this forest, this holy ground were joining me in my quest for healing.

I have heard Donna say many uplifting and inspiring things during the years of our being together, but never had I heard something so beautiful, so inspired, and so authentic. Then I knew why we had flown from Spokane all the way to San Francisco to come to Muir Woods on this day, to park in that spot, and to stand on this plot of land in the company of giants.

I hugged Donna among the trees.

There's a quote I love from author Martha Beck that seems appropriate at this point: "If you allow it, your life will flow into zones of astonishment you could never invent."

The key word in Martha's quote for me is *allow*. I was looking to the redwoods to deliver a life-changing message to me. My attention was solely focused on the trees. But in demanding the trees convey what I wanted to hear, I was not allowing another voice, one so close to me, so obvious, to speak at the right and perfect moment.

As Jesus was riding into Jerusalem on a donkey, people threw palm fronds before him and cheered. "Blessed is the one who comes in the name of the Lord" (Matthew 21:9). There were scribes and Pharisees in the crowd who yelled at Jesus to shut up the crowd. Jesus replied, "I tell you, if these were silent, the stones would shout out" (Luke 19:40).

It reminded me of that Seahawks game where the decibel count of cheering fans went off the chart. There was a message behind that cheering. And it could not be shut up.

I began to appreciate the many voices that were now cheering me on—the 12s, the trees, and most of all, my life companion, not to mention Radiance, Turk, and all my mechanical helpers back home.

Threads for Discussion --

1. Where do you go or whom do you turn to when you seek guidance or an answer to some challenging situation?

2. Are you a lover of trees, or is there some other part of nature you commune with?

3. What part of nature has spoken to you most often?

4. Are you currently allowing your life to flow into "zones of astonishment"?

A CLOAK OF MANY COLORS

Chapter 8

Now Israel loved Joseph more than all his
children, because he was the son of his old age:
and he made him a coat of many colors. —Genesis
37:3 KJV

One of my favorite Old Testament characters is Joseph, one of the 12 sons of Jacob/Israel. (There's that number 12 again that keeps popping up.) From what I gather from the Bible, while Jacob loved all his sons, he loved Joseph the most. Joseph is described as the son of Jacob's old age. He loved him so much that he made him an ornamental robe that came to be known as "the coat of many colors." In modern times—the year 1982, to be exact—there was a Broadway musical production called *Joseph and the Amazing Technicolor Dreamcoat*, and later a movie.

The reason I love Joseph's story so much is because his story lends itself so well to some of my early biblical training in what is called metaphysical Bible interpretation. In a nutshell, it means that while some of the stories in the Bible happened as historical events, all the stories have an esoteric or symbolic meaning that applies to our everyday life.

And so I invite you to explore with me the possibility that Joseph's coat of many colors represents something that is an integral part of ourselves—a part that brings color, variety, and possibility directly into our lives. The part that Joseph represents is the amazing, technicolor power of our own imagination. Isn't it our imagination that brings, among other things, color, variety, and infinite possibilities into our lives? And maybe this includes healing too.

We also learn that Joseph was a dreamer. He knew how to interpret dreams—his own and others'. Dreams allow us to go to places we've only dreamed of. Dreams remove the limits and boundaries from our lives. We can walk on air! We can fly! And if you're like Joseph, your dreams can result in your becoming very powerful.

As children, our first and favorite pastime is to develop an activity called daydreaming. We all love to imagine ourselves in other places, at other times, doing and being things that only our imagination can create for us.

However, there is a downside to an overactive imagination. It can get us into trouble. It can lead to nightmares, worry, fear, and being thrown into a deep, dark pit. That is what happened to Joseph when he began to share his dreams with his brothers. They threw him into a pit and eventually sold him into slavery in Egypt.

As I am writing these words, I am thinking about the bizarre ride my imagination took when I was told I had only a few months to live. I found myself in the pits. I found myself enslaved by a body that was going to kill me and do it sooner rather than later. I felt trapped with no way out.

But imagination can always show us a way out as well as a way through. While in prison in Egypt, Joseph was called upon to interpret the dreams of the Pharaoh, the supreme leader of the Egyptians.

Joseph's amazing interpretation so impressed Pharaoh that he made Joseph second in command in the land and gave him the job of making sure the Egyptian people, who were headed toward seven years of famine, made the most of the years before the famine, the years of plenty.

I was certain that the situation I found myself in had not only imprisoned me but immersed me and my dear Donna in a physical famine with all our resources, which, when tallied up, would prove to be insufficient not only to stave off the cancer but all the imagined aftermath that my death would leave behind. I found myself living in a way in which my dire diagnosis had locked me up for good. I could see no way out.

Despite the amazing cheering section my imagination had created—despite the prayers, the praise, the possibilities that lay before me—I was still feeling like a victim of circumstances, chained to the limits of a body that was fast deteriorating.

Then one day a package arrived. I opened it and, to my surprise, what I saw was a multicolored blanket—yes, you could say a sort of "coat of many colors." The return address on the package was from a woman in Philadelphia. She said she was a friend of my nephew Andy.

Andy, who lives in Ontario, Canada, made regular visits to Philadelphia to conduct a session of what he called "shaking." Do not ask me to explain what goes on at a "shake," but it is a spiritual practice where people gyrate and vibrate into a space of spiritual awareness and healing. As I understand it, its modern use was developed by Bradford Keeney, Ph.D., in which "shaking" is used as a healing modality. Andy had a group of about 30 in Philly.

At one of his "shakes" he mentioned to the group that his Uncle David (that's me) was seriously ill with "incurable cancer," and he wanted to do whatever he could to bring about a transformation for me.

So he had the group "shake" and then he took out this many-colored blanket and had each one touch it and bless it. Then he passed it on to the woman I mentioned earlier. She was instructed to mail it to me and explain the process the group had gone through to prepare this "technicolor dreamcoat" for me.

I was overjoyed to receive this gift. I wrapped the blanket around me, and it wasn't long before I began to feel an energy I had not felt before. Interestingly, when Donna later had colon cancer, she too wrapped herself in the cloak of many colors and found the same healing energy within the blanket.

Back to the story of Joseph. His brothers, by this time in the throes of the famine, ate some humble pie and came to Egypt with hat in hand for an audience with their brother. They asked him for some of his stockpiled food—supplies that would get them through the famine.

Joseph willingly and generously gave them a ton of food, plus their money back. And his parting words to his brothers who had thrown him in a pit were, "Even though you intended to do harm to me, God intended it for good" (Genesis 50:20).

What I learned from this is that, even when I believe my body is out to destroy me, there is an energy at work that can turn things around. We can all start imagining ourselves as whole, perfect, and complete. We can all wear our coat of many colors and dream a possible dream.

Threads for Discussion

1. Joseph in the Bible represents the power of the imagination. This is a power within each one of us. We can use it to envision ourselves whole. We can use it to see life in our body instead of that which limits life. How are you using the power of your imagination these days?

2. Are your dreams vivid enough to remember after you awaken? Are they vivid enough to write them down? Do they send any messages to you?

3. Have you ever felt you were in a deep, dark pit or a prison? How did you free yourself?

4. Is there someone or something that is calling for your mercy and your forgiveness, like Joseph gave his brothers?

5. Do you feel that sometimes the One you might call God has intervened on your behalf, or is it something you did to attract good into your life?

A CALL FROM ACROSS THE SEA

Chapter 9

Hawaii is "the loveliest fleet of islands that lies anchored in any ocean."—Mark Twain

When I was growing up in Toronto we lived in a duplex in the east end of the city. Our home was small but certainly big enough for our family, which consisted of my mom and dad, my brothers Donald and Bobby, my sister Karen, and me.

Every evening after supper, we would gather around my dad's prized possession: a tall Philips console radio. We would listen to the news, sports, and *Fibber McGee and Molly*. On weekends, we would tune in to *Let's Pretend* and *The Green Hornet*.

On Sunday afternoons, we listened to a most beautiful program titled *Hawaii Calls*. It was a live broadcast that came across the sea from Hawaii, then beamed across the North American continent to our little home in Toronto. The program featured a charming commentator by the name of Webley Edwards, Hawaiian music, the sound of the sea, and the twang of Hawaiian guitars and ukuleles. We fell in love with that show. Sometimes my mother would get up and give her version of a hula dance to a welcoming and appreciative audience.

I think that's where I first fell in love with Hawaii. I loved it so much that when an opportunity came to apply as minister at the Unity Church of Hawaii in Honolulu, Donna and I jumped at the chance. More about our Hawaiian threads later. I want to share the most important call I ever got from our beloved islands.

Fast-forward to a chilly December afternoon in Spokane in 2014, after my cancer diagnosis. My cell phone rang and I heard the familiar voice of Jon DeLuca, a friend who was serving on the board of Unity Windward church, a ministry where Donna and I had served back in the early 2000s. He had been on the board of directors when we were ministering there. By trade, he owned and ran a swimming pool maintenance business in Kailua. I was surprised when he called me here on the mainland.

We chatted for a while and exchanged memories and niceties. Then he asked how I was feeling. He was one of the members of my 12th Person Healing Team and knew that I was going through treatment for Stage 4 metastatic melanoma. I told him I was at a low place in my life, undergoing a series of dates with my radiation machine, a.k.a. Radiance. I told him about taking my current cancer infusion, which consisted of some horrible drug that was giving me rashes all over my body and not helping my melanoma one bit.

He listened compassionately and then asked, "Have you ever heard of an immunotherapy drug called Keytruda?"

I said that I had not. I asked him to elaborate on this strange-sounding substance. He told me the Merck pharmaceutical company, which developed this drug, had started clinical trials aimed specifically toward the treatment of melanoma.

Then he told me a story about a client of his, someone whose swimming pool was cleaned and serviced. As he understood it, this client had the exact same diagnosis I was laboring under—Stage 4 metastatic melanoma. He said his client decided to sign up for a clinical trial for Keytruda that was underway in Atlanta, Georgia. He went every three weeks for an infusion of the drug.

I couldn't believe what I was hearing. "You mean to tell me that this guy gets on an airplane in Honolulu and flies to Atlanta, Georgia, every three weeks just for a shot of this trial immunotherapy drug?"

My friend said, "Yep! That is what I'm telling you. And he has been doing this now for a year, and—now here's the good part—his cancer is gone, free and clear!"

I don't know how long the pause in the conversation lasted that afternoon. But it was *long*. I could not find words to grasp the significance of what I had just been told. My friend was a bit of a jokester, and we loved to kid around with each other.

Finally, I asked him to repeat what he had just told me. Again, he said, "This guy has been on Keytruda—one infusion every three weeks for a year—and his Stage 4 metastatic melanoma is kaput! Gone! Vanished! Healed!"

He followed that up by saying, "And so, David, you need to get yourself down to Atlanta pronto and get you some of that 'joy juice.'"

Finally, the impact of what he was telling me registered. A guy with *my* cancer was taking a new trial drug and his cancer was completely gone.

I called Donna to the phone and had her talk to my friend, just to be sure I had not misheard his words or been talking to some snake-oil salesman. Her face lit up with a glow I had not seen in months. She nodded to me that there was nothing wrong with my hearing and that what I had heard was true.

After a lot of *thank you's* and *mahalo's* and *yippee's*, I bid him *aloha* and said I would contact Merck immediately to join the trial. I knew it would mean a major expense for us, having to fly to Atlanta every three weeks from Spokane, but it was a ray of sunshine in the clouds and there was no doubt this was a step I must take—and take now.

Threads for Discussion

1. Have you ever had an unexpected and unplanned-for door open before you with a glorious solution to a long-standing problem? How did you handle it?

2. If you were told there was a solution to a challenge in your life that seemed impossible to solve, what would you think?

3. How far would you go to receive a complete healing of a situation you were certain could not be remedied?

HAVE YOU SEEN THE MORNING PAPER?
Chapter 10

We are all beads strung together on the same
thread of love.—Mata Amritanandamayi

After my beloved Hawaii called, with heaps of hope and the promise of a way out of my darkness, I hurriedly contacted Merck, the pharmaceutical giant in Atlanta. Yes, they did have a trial currently underway for Keytruda. And yes, I could apply to be a part of the trial. And no, I could not join the trial now, as there was quite a waiting list. But yes, they would put me on the wait list and let me know when I had been accepted into the trial.

I had pictured getting on the next plane to Atlanta and starting my test of this new "joy juice," as my friend had named it. Instead, I had to tell myself, *Cool your jets, Davey-Boy!*

This drug, which is not chemotherapy but immunotherapy, has the generic name of pembrolizumab. On the Merck website, I found this about the drug. Note the words *death* and *fatal* throughout the description:

> KEYTRUDA is a monoclonal antibody that belongs to a class of drugs that bind to either the programmed death receptor-1 (PD-1) or the programmed death ligand 1 (PD-L1), blocking the PD-1/PD-L1 pathway, thereby removing inhibition of the immune response, potentially breaking peripheral tolerance and inducing immune-mediated adverse reactions.
>
> Immune-mediated adverse reactions, which may be severe or fatal, can occur in any organ system or tissue, can affect more than one body system simultaneously, and can occur at any time after starting treatment or after discontinuation of treatment.

> Important immune-mediated adverse reactions
> listed here may not include all possible severe and
> fatal immune-mediated adverse reactions.

This did not make me any more hopeful.

The more I thought about taking, at a minimum, six months out of my life to try this so-far-untried drug seemed highly impractical and not very appealing. I was still fully employed as the senior minister at Unity in Spokane. That was one thing. Then there was the expense of flying to and from Atlanta every three weeks. And so much more!

The open door to the possibility of a cure for my cancer had seemed overwhelmingly exciting when my Hawaiian friend shared the information, especially since his client was now supposedly cancer-free. But when it came down to the practicality of it all, and the leap of faith it would require of me, I had to take some time to pray about my next steps.

Weeks went by without a word from Merck. I busied myself with the tasks at hand—being a preacher, teacher, and husband. Donna continued her work as a chaplain at Sacred Heart Medical Center, and life, such as it was, went on.

It was September 4, 2014, on what started out to be a normal day, with the only distinguishing characteristics being that it was a crisp, bright, sunny day and four days short of my 77th birthday. I drove to the church office as usual. I unlocked my office door and walked in.

I had scarcely gotten to my desk to sit down when Rev. Jackie Green, the youth education director and a longtime friend, rushed into my office.

She said, "I have been waiting for you! Have you seen the morning paper?"

I told her, "No, I don't get the morning paper. I get all my news from TV."

Then she plunked a copy of *The Spokesman-Review*, Spokane's premier newspaper, down on my desk.

"Take a look at this," she said. "It's right on the front page! As bold as it can be! Someone really wanted to get your attention, David!"

I looked at the top page of the news sheet before me, and there it was. "Breakthrough cancer drug approved by the FDA."

At first it didn't register with me what I was reading. But then I read on:

"Merck ... today announced that the U.S. Food and Drug Administration (FDA) has approved KEYTRUDA® (pembrolizumab) at a dose of 2 mg/kg every three weeks for the treatment of patients with unresectable or metastatic melanoma and disease progression following ipilimumab and, if BRAF V600 mutation positive, a BRAF inhibitor. This indication is approved under accelerated approval based on tumor response rate and durability of response."

The paper in my hand began to shake as I read and reread the headline and the details repeatedly. And then it finally sank in. There was hope! There was more than hope—there was a possibility. Not only had Keytruda been taken out of its experimental phase, but it would presumably be available everywhere without special trips to Atlanta.

I could feel the healing thread encircling me and wrapping itself around my body and my whole being. There, staring at me from the front page of this newspaper, was a new door opening before me. The clouds were beginning to part. And my heart was jumping for joy!

I can't quite remember, but I think I hugged Jackie profusely and thanked her even more profusely for being the harbinger of this life-transforming news. I grabbed my keys, told Jackie I would be back whenever, and drove home to share the news with Donna.

We danced, we cried, we skipped, we flipped! My sleep that evening was like no sleep I had had in months.

The next day, it just so happened that I had a regularly scheduled appointment with my oncologist at Cancer Care Northwest. He had taken me off another drug that had been having horrendous effects on my body, with severe rashes, pain, and other tortures.

He had said, "It's killing you quicker than the cancer is. At the rate we're going, David, you have only a couple weeks to live."

The PET scans at the time revealed the cancer was not only *not* going away but was metastasizing to far-reaching parts of my anatomy at an alarming rate. My oncologist shared pictures of these scans, and what I saw looked like a Christmas tree with multicolored lights lighting up various and sundry parts of my anatomy—each light an indication of cancer. Not only was this not a sign of Christmas, it was a sign my days on planet Earth were numbered.

But on this day, I bounced into his office, newspaper clipping in hand, and I barely got in his door when he came waltzing in with the very same newspaper clipping in his hand. We laughed! We cried! We hugged! We celebrated!

Then he said, "Okay, David. Let's get down to business. And the first order of business is to find out if your body has the right elements to receive this drug." He went on to say that, from what he had read, in order for Keytruda to be effective, one must have what is called a BRAF inhibitor. He said there was a simple test to find out if I had this all-important element within me.

I said, "When do we begin?"

"I will arrange for a test immediately," he said, "and we should know the results in a week."

A week later, I was back in his office. Before he could say anything, I saw the grin on his face. "You have the BRAF, David!" he announced. "So now we must fit you with a port." He explained it was a device surgically placed in the chest through which they would administer the Keytruda infusion directly into my bloodstream.

A few days later, I was given my port and was ready for my first infusion of "joy juice." As you remember, I became proficient at giving inanimate things a name, and so Keytruda (pembrolizumab) came to be known by me and the amazing nurses in the Chemo Lounge as "The Juice of Joy!" I was told I was the first person in Spokane to receive this new drug. Since then, thousands have been blessed and have benefited from this drug even as you read these words. Please know that this is not to say it works for everyone, because it doesn't. But it works for many who, like me, had lost all hope of turning things around.

Threads for Discussion ————————————————————

1. Have you ever been in a situation where you felt that all hope was lost? How did you feel and what did you do about it?

2. Have you ever been in a situation when, despite all that was going against you, an unexpected, amazing, astonishing thing happened that changed everything? What happened and how did you respond?

3. Are you open to good news? What would be the best news you could receive?

LET THE JOY JUICE FLOW

Chapter 11

*Today healing energy constantly flows through
every organ, joint, and cell in my body.*—Louise Hay

After two months of Keytruda infusions—once every three weeks in Spokane—I had another PET scan. This one indicated that some of the "Christmas tree lights" in my body were not as merry and bright as they had been previously. The doctor was hopeful this indicated progress.

Two months later, another scan. And another dimming of the bright, cancerous lights in my kidneys, lungs, spine, and other parts of my body.

Finally, after six months of joy-juicing every three weeks, I had another scan. The doctor led Donna and me over to his computer so we could see the pictures. There were my inner organs where they were supposed to be. There was my skeleton intact. And there was the most amazing sight I had ever seen! No lights. Which meant (are you ready for this?) *no cancer!*

It was completely gone. Not a trace remained. I looked at Donna and we cried together.

I looked at my friend the oncologist and said, "Does this mean what I think it means?"

He said, "David, I am happy to say to you that, yes, it does!"

I hugged him and we laughed together.

There is no question that this was the happiest day of my life! Truly, I could say that there are astonishing things that can take place when you allow the healing thread to do its work.

I could not wait to get home and call my family and let them know the news. That Sunday, I announced it to a standing ovation from the congregation. I emailed all my 12s and thanked them profusely for making this day of healing possible. It had been about 15 months since my initial dire diagnosis.

Although the cancer was gone, the doctor said he would still recommend I take my "joy juice" every three weeks. He said that because Keytruda was such a new drug, they had no research on how long a patient should stay on it once they were completely cancer-free.

And so, every three weeks, I religiously (if you'll pardon the pun) went to the clinic to continue taking Keytruda. I ended up doing this for almost seven more years. Today, I no longer infuse and, according to my latest scan, the cancer has never returned.

What do I want to say to you about this transformation that has taken place in my body and in my life? What I want to say to you are the words that the Mother of Unity said more than a century ago: *I am a child of God, and therefore I do not inherit sickness.*

These are not words from the past. They are and always will be words that are the truth about you and me—yesterday, today, and on into infinity. It's a truth that you can take with you into any situation. You could easily say, *I am a child of God, and therefore I do not inherit poverty or loneliness or any other limiting human condition.*

Knowing that you are a chip off the divine block is to know your strength, your resilience, your overcoming power.

I want to address right here and now that there is always a balance of spiritual and medical healing that combines to bring about transformation. Mother Myrtle healed herself with prayer and I attempted to follow her principles. At the same time I sought out Western medicine and used everything it had to offer, which is considerably more than in Myrtle's day. I do not know the details of what medical means Myrtle tried, but I believe that it's okay to use one or both. Healing is a spiritual journey even if it includes surgery and drug treatments.

So that's my healing story and I'm sticking to it!

I want to quickly say that not all people who take Keytruda have the same results. Some have severe side effects, and some do not see their cancer go away. It's imperative to work through a qualified oncologist and lab. While many have been helped and healed by this drug, individual cases are not always the same. But since that first trial, Keytruda has been used as a treatment for at least 14 types of cancer beyond melanoma.

My many thanks to the folks at Merck; at Cancer Care Northwest; my 12th Man healing prayer team; my friend in Hawaii, Jon DeLuca; and most of all my inspirational wife, Donna, who held on to the unifying threads of heart and mind when I found it hard to keep my grip on these threads. When I thought the Seahawks had lost the game, the 12s kept me in the game!

The all-loving, all-powerful healing thread within me truly has had my back throughout this entire adventure, giving me more time on planet Earth. I am using most of this gift of time to document my healing and the myriad ways these unifying threads of heart and mind have shown themselves since the very day of my birth.

Dear friend, know that the healing thread (or whatever name you choose to call the healing God of your being) is with you right now and always. It will work with you, through you, for you, and around you to bless the life you are living. It can restore and renew you!

Threads for Discussion --

1. Have you or a loved one experienced a significant, life-threatening condition?

2. Have you or a loved one received medical treatment that healed or diminished the effects of the condition?

3. What is your current state of mind concerning your health? If you are not already healed, are you still hopeful for a healing? How do you define *healing*?

THE HEALING THREAD CONTINUES
Chapter 12

*We don't accomplish anything in this world
alone ... and whatever happens is the result of the
whole tapestry of one's life and all the weavings of
individual threads from one to another that creates
something.* — Sandra Day O'Connor

To demonstrate to you that healing can and does happen in amazing ways, I want to share a sequel to my story.

I resigned as the senior minister of Unity Spiritual Center of Spokane (as it is now called) in 2015. Although I was now cancer-free, I felt I needed to step aside and let someone else take on the duties and responsibilities of this large, energetic ministry on Spokane's South Hill.

I remained their Sunday morning speaker for a bit longer while they began an earnest and prayerful search for a replacement. The church formed a search team. I remember strongly urging them, as they prayed for a new minister, to use some version of the prayer that had guided me throughout my ministerial career. That prayer was, of course, *Here am I, Lord. Use me.* Their version was slightly different, *Here we are, Lord. Guide us!* This prayer unites the healing thread with its partner, the guiding thread, which opens the mind of the one praying to amazing and miraculous guidance. This prayer takes one to "headquarters" just as it guided Charles Fillmore to bring Unity to the world.

The only criteria I laid down to the board of directors and search team was that whomever they chose for the position of senior minister must be revealed to them by the guiding thread or whatever they wanted to call the Higher Power, and not by convenience, politics, and familiarity. I had seen too many ministries jump into making choices that did not serve their best interests because they had not prayerfully selected the succession of leadership.

Within a year, they made what turned out to be a wise and perfect choice—it was not one minister but a married man and woman, Revs. Drs. Gary and Jane Simmons, both ordained Unity ministers. They were hired and welcomed into Unity Spiritual Center Spokane.

I was then awarded the honor of becoming minister emeritus. I remained in close contact with the ministry, teaching classes and filling in on Sundays when the ministers were out of town.

And then a most profound event took place. Gary Simmons announced to the congregation one Sunday that he had been diagnosed with (are you ready for this?) Stage 4 metastatic melanoma. Nearly the same diagnosis I had three years earlier.

In talking with him recently, he gave a clear account of his healing process. He has given me permission to quote him. This is what he told me:

> Yes, I had melanoma, a rare form of internal skin cancer that spread throughout my body (more than 30 tumors). I started dosing medical cannabis 30 days prior to my first Keytruda infusion. I was cancer-free by my third Keytruda infusion, much to the amazement of my oncologist. I was in complete remission 60 days after my diagnosis. My oncologist had never seen such a rapid remission. He supported my medical authorization allowing me to grow my own medicine.
>
> I am now more than seven years in remission, no longer a cancer patient. My current family doctor has told me not to stop with the cannabis as it will return. "Keep doing what you are doing," he declared.

Was this a coincidence or was this gentleman also a part of the same healing thread I had found in my healing? This question proved to be even more intriguing in that I had first encountered Gary in San Francisco while ministering at a Unity church there in the 1970s. His then father-in-law had been president of the church board there. Later, Gary decided he would enter the

Unity ministerial training program to become a minister himself. Coincidence or synchronicity? I believe that the unifying thread was weaving its way through our lives to bring us together so that we could share our healing adventure.

Over the years, Gary and I had worked on various Unity committees together, and he assisted in helping me make peace in a couple of rambunctious ministries where I was serving. Now here he was, showing up in the ministry where I had threads galore, only to follow almost the same healing path that was mine to follow.

Yet, since the initial news that I was cancer-free, I have experienced a few other bodily challenges.

For example, I spent a week in the hospital in 2020 with Covid. I was told mine was a "difficult and serious" case. I was put in isolation and kept under close supervision. Fortunately, I was not put on a respirator and soon began to regain my strength. Within a week, I was discharged and spent a couple of weeks recuperating at home, discovering that my ability to walk had left me.

I quickly enrolled in a physical therapy course where it took several weeks to regain my motor skills. My constant prayer, here again, was Momma Myrtle's: *I am a child of God, and therefore I do not inherit sickness.*

I was never quite sure whether the word *inherit* meant the same as *catch*, but I knew that my healing came from within. And, more than ever before, I knew that the one I have come to know as the healing thread has always and will always have my back. During my recuperation period, I found my strength and my trust in Spirit within me to continue to do its healing work.

My faith that I was indeed a child of God and did not inherit sickness would be tested once again. Early in 2022, I came down with a god-awful thing called pancreatitis, which occurs when digestive enzymes become activated while still in the pancreas, irritating the cells of your pancreas and causing inflammation. Something like that.

That was no fun at all, and I don't wish it on anybody. Back to the hospital with me! Another week of mostly pain and misery. I was sorely tempted to ask myself: *Is my faith waning? Am I inheriting something that didn't come from someone else but from my own consciousness?*

By the time I got out of the hospital eight days later, I could not walk again. I was relegated to a wheelchair and brought home. Thankfully, a group of friends, folks who remained members of my 12th Person Healing Team, were there when I was wheeled from the car to our apartment.

I immediately signed up once again for physical therapy with a woman I had worked with over the years when I was recovering from cancer. She literally had to teach me to walk again.

I soon graduated to a walker, and later you could see me walking around with the assistance of a cane. Today, I walk on my own two legs without assistance. I do have to watch my balance and try as best I can to stay clear of our rampaging kittens as they tear around the apartment. So far, so good.

My Keytruda treatments ended. And the healing thread continued working in and through me.

Threads for Discussion ————————————————————

1. What have been your prevailing bodily ailments or symptoms over the years? Do you still have some of these physical problems or have they disappeared?

2. Have you been able to maintain your faith in the healing thread through all your changes and challenges?

3. What has been your guiding light?

4. Do you have a sense that you are being guided during your life?

I'LL SHOW YOU MINE, DONNA, IF YOU'LL SHOW ME YOURS

Chapter 13

And I will show that there is no imperfection in the
present, and can be none in the future,
And I will show that whatever happens to anybody
it may be turn'd to beautiful results,
And I will show that nothing can happen more
beautiful than death,
And I will thread a thread
through my poems that time and events are
compact,
And that all the things of the universe are perfect
miracles, each as profound as any.—Walt Whitman

The light of the healing/guiding threads entwine and wrap themselves around every soul on planet Earth. They continue to shine in and through me and you and all by themselves are enough to guide and support every one of us. They are totally responsible for helping me in the writing of this book. I am so grateful that I can get around with little or no concern. Pretty good for a child of God who, in human years, is almost 86 as I write this.

I have been pretty much able to return to what has been mine to do for my entire adult life—preach and teach—mostly on a part-time basis, and now I have added writing to my daily activities. This book, which I started in 2014, is now being created with new time, enthusiasm, and wisdom that I did not have back then.

Just when I felt as though I had regained my health and gotten my act together, the spotlight turned toward my dear wife, Donna.

Donna had her own dance with Covid. Hers was a much milder form than mine, and she recovered quickly. But she went through other health adventures that now prompted her to invoke Myrtle

Fillmore's epic words: *I am a child of God, and therefore I do not inherit sickness.*

Within a span of five years, between 2011 and 2016, Donna was diagnosed twice with breast cancer. In both cases, a simple dissection of the tumors and radiation took care of it for her. Happily, she did not lose her breasts. Instead, she gained an increased measure of faith and strength, which would prepare her for what lay ahead. Cancer was not finished with her yet.

In 2021, a routine scan revealed she had Stage 3 metastatic colon cancer. This was a much more aggressive and widespread cancer that, if not checked, would spell an early end to her journey on Earth. Oh, wow. Here we go again!

And so, once again and again and again, there were Mother Myrtle's words ringing in our ears: *I am a child of God, and therefore I do not inherit sickness.*

Both Donna and I had family members who had cancer—my grandmother and Donna's father. Myrtle's quote is so powerful to both of us because we have always joked about being "chips off the family block." We would catch ourselves every now and then when we noticed a trait that could be directly traced to one of our blood family members. Both of us had to take genealogy tests prior to our cancer treatment. Even knowing our family connections to cancer, we both staunchly held to our relationship with the healing thread.

Donna's first step was to find a skilled, competent oncologist. Once again, we turned to the guiding thread, which led us back to Cancer Care Northwest (CCNW), which had been so instrumental in my recovery. She was directed to a newly hired oncologist who had just joined the cancer team at their Valley Clinic. My super oncologist practiced at the South Hill Clinic, which was a stone's throw from where we lived. To get to the Valley, five miles from our home, required some assistance from the volunteer arm of CCNW, who gave their time and use of their vehicles to transport patients to and from their treatments in the Valley.

The new oncologist evaluated, scanned, and concluded that Donna did indeed have colon cancer and that an aggressive six-month series of chemotherapy infusions would be required. When Donna asked what the prospects of this treatment were—would it destroy the cancer or would it simply slow it down?—the doctor's amazing reply was, "Donna, we are going for a healing here—nothing less!"

However, the oncologist was quick to inform Donna that she would most likely experience severe side effects from the drug she would be receiving. Among these would be fatigue, hair-thinning, nausea, and possible peripheral neuropathy, nerve damage that can cause pain and numbness.

Here began a rigorous and difficult chapter in dear Donna's life, as she began to take regular trips with the team of volunteers to the Valley CCNW. Over the next six months, Donna dutifully showed up for her treatments and took her medicine while keeping a steady, positive attitude.

Just as the doctor had predicted, the side effects began to visit Donna's body. It was hard on her, I could tell, but she was determined to persevere. She was not just hoping for the best. She was *claiming* her divine connection with the healing thread.

During Donna's treatment, there emerged her own version of the 12th person healing team, which came into being to assist both of us in this new recovery process.

This team consisted of many of those who had supported me during my healing, but now it included an amazing "food train" that delivered much-appreciated meals to our home twice a week for many months.

Donna also received amazing support from her brother, Paul, and his wife, Charlyn, in Arizona. In addition, Donna's fellow chaplains at the hospital united in their spiritual and physical support in very generous ways.

Finally, in the summer of 2022 after a thorough examination and scan, Donna was pronounced cancer-free and clear. Cancer no longer lived in her body. Having grown up with a great family affiliation with Unity, she had always affirmed that she was indeed a child of God and knew deep down inside that her true self would not allow sickness to remain. Within a few months, Donna had regained her strength and returned on a limited basis to her job as chaplain at Sacred Heart Medical Center.

There were many lessons Donna learned from this experience—some of the same lessons I had been learning. Although we were now both cancer-free and healthy, we soon discovered that we were not as skippy, perky, and frisky as we had been in our younger years. But much to our joy and gratitude, there were still many things we could accomplish, singly and together. There was so much that we could contribute, serve, inspire, and bring to others.

To this day, Donna still serves as a hospital chaplain a few days a week. She remains a member of the prayer team at Unity Spiritual Center of Spokane and prays with those who are seeking their own healing. Though she tires more quickly than she used to, she is still available to help, support, and pray with dozens of patients at the hospital.

So, with the strength, enthusiasm, resourcefulness, and faith we both still have, we continue to share with our community, friends, and family.

I asked Donna what lessons she learned from her healing experience:

- She learned that, just because her cancer is gone, her complete healing from side effects is still ongoing. She knows that although the road ahead is clear, she must walk the road at a slower pace than she did before.
- She is filled with gratitude for all those who came to her aid and support—fellow chaplains, people driving her to medical appointments and treatments, and the food train that formed around us.

To say our hearts are grateful to have returned to some measure of wholeness and health would be an understatement.

Threads for Discussion

1. Have you ever had someone near and dear to you going through a similar healing adventure as you? What was the outcome?

2. If you have had or are in the process of an illness, do you have a family history of this illness? Who in your family has gone through the same illness?

3. Did you have regular and sustained treatments for your illness? How far did you have to travel for these treatments?

4. Did you ever have any relapses or did you reach a point where total healing was reached?

Part Two

THE GUIDING THREAD

A TAPESTRY BEGINS BY WEAVING THREADS
Chapter 14

*Destiny itself is like a wonderful broad tapestry
where every thread is in woven by an infinitely
delicate hand, laid next to its fellow, and held and
supported by a hundred others.* —Rainer Maria Rilke

I originally planned to write this book in chronological order. But those wiser in book-writing advised me to put the "big kahuna"— our healing journeys—front and center, since they are the main threads behind all that has taken place in our lives.

I started writing back in 2014, soon after my remission from cancer. However, at some point, I realized it was in my best interests to step back, pick up some of my earlier threads, and see how the tapestry of my life had unfolded and transformed itself. I trust that the order I have put my chapters allows me to continue sharing this amazing journey with you as I thread and weave my way from there to here.

In the introduction, I outlined the threads of oneness that I now believe began with the Australian Aboriginals, at least for this planet. From there, the earliest strands began to form part of an even more expansive tapestry that runs through you, me, and everyone. This is the tapestry that reveals our true and eternal spiritual identity and the journey that is our lives.

Ralph Waldo Emerson, the transcendentalist writer in the mid-1800s, helped usher in the beginnings of what would eventually be called the New Thought movement. Among the early leaders of the movement were Mary Baker Eddy, who founded Christian Science in 1879; Emma Curtis Hopkins, one of Eddy's students who set up her own school, where her students included Charles and Myrtle Fillmore, who founded Unity in 1889; and Ernest Holmes, who published *The Science of Mind* in 1926.

In 1913 an event happened in Spokane, Washington, that would change the world, extending the thread of what was called *New Thought* to the far reaches of North America and beyond.

This was a thread that would bring Donna and me together and extend our relationship to this very day and all our days beyond.

It started with a gentleman by the name of Dr. Albert C. Grier, who founded what he called the Church of Truth here in Spokane. His aim was to create a place that would heal the "total human" (mind, body, and soul) and thus create a full awakening of what he called "the Christ within." This ministry was initially called The Church of Truth, then Unity Church of Truth, and finally today, in its newer location, Unity Spiritual Center Spokane, where Donna and I met, married, and to this day call our home ministry.

In his amazing ministerial career, Grier founded 22 Churches of Truth in North America. He became a major influence in the early New Thought movement, working closely with other prominent leaders of his day such as Ernest Holmes, who founded Religious Science in 1927, and leaders in both the Eastern and Western traditions. He taught physical, mental, and spiritual healing through the knowledge and practical application of what he called universal principles.

And so as we continue to weave the tapestry of my life, Donna's, and many others all over the world, I want to explore more fully the second of the two threads that compose the one unifying thread. This I call the *guiding thread*. It has led me to an awesome series of adventures.

As you've heard me say throughout this book, there is one unifying thread that has two characteristics or offshoots—a healing thread that has its source in our innermost heart, and a guiding thread that is connected to our mind. These dual threads contain all the possibilities that you and I will ever need for everything in our lives here on planet Earth. These, I believe are the basic Mother and Father of all creation. In our body temple we experience these threads as feeling and thinking. These threads have always been there for and with you. They were there before your birth and are, right now, even as you read these words, connecting you to the Source of All Life—the One that, at the risk of continuing to repeat myself, you know as the unifying thread.

To catch where these threads began for me, let me now take you back to my very birth this time around on planet Earth.

Threads for Discussion ————————————————————————————

1. Share where your spiritual journey began and how it has led you to pick up this book.
2. Where would you place the origins of the idea that there is one presence and one power in the universe? Or a sense that we are all one?
3. Where do you think your own spiritual thread is leading you now?
4. What is something you know with all your heart and all your mind?

I WAS BORN AT SANTA'S HALFWAY HOUSE
Chapter 15

*One who believes he is influenced by others forgets
his birthright: forgets that he is the child of God and
free from all limitation.* —Emma Curtis Hopkins

I was born on September 8, 1937, in a small town called Bracebridge, which is situated about 100 miles north of Toronto, Ontario, Canada. My parents lived about 15 miles from Bracebridge on a beautiful lake called Mary, in the small village of Port Sydney.

Bracebridge's claim to fame (besides the place of my birth) is that it is situated geographically exactly halfway between the North Pole and the equator—"Santa's Stopping Off Place on Christmas Eve," the Bracebridgers love to claim.

And so, for whatever reason, I was basically born on the 45th parallel north, which means that during the summer months, I was living in a powerful position in regard to what would become my dear, old friend and most formidable challenge—Old Sól. You might not think that Ontario has much powerful sunlight, but let me tell you, in July and August the highs can get into the 80s up there!

The first evidence I have that the unifying thread has always had my back came a few days after I came into the world. I was diagnosed with jaundice. This may not seem like an instance of the healing thread, but wait, there's more!

Today, while jaundice is still a serious medical problem, especially for newborns, back then the midwife told my parents that my time on the planet would be limited to a few weeks or maybe a month. But thanks to good genes or mother's milk, I pulled through with flying colors and began my journey into the great adventure of this life. Eventually our family moved permanently to Toronto, but we still maintained a summer cottage on Mary Lake. During the summer, every day and sometimes three times a day, I would walk the 100 yards from our lake cottage to the town dock, where I would roll out my towel and plunk my pure white Canadian body down on the wooden planks of the dock and resume baking in the sun.

In those days, suntans were all the rage. But you had to start out with a dandy sunburn first—ouch! After a few days, my skin would reach the preferred medium brown color, and I became a cool dude with a million-dollar tan. I would not say that I had to beat the girls off with a stick, but I did okay in that department.

Although my mother always warned me about getting too much sun and scolded me when I burned to a crisp, I have always been a sun-lover at heart.

As mentioned, our family moved to the big city of Toronto where, when I was 7, those amazing, unifying threads of heart and mind began to unfurl and weave themselves through not only our family ties but ties I could not have imagined.

My mother, Norma, who was originally from Rochester, New York, had a sister living in New York City. Aunt Hazel was a stenographer. In those days, there were no computers or recording equipment, so everything had to be taken down in what was called shorthand.

Aunt Hazel had been hearing about a minister by the name of Emmet Fox, who was lecturing to overflow crowds at Carnegie Hall in Manhattan. She decided to go check out Fox one Sunday and came away a different woman. So taken was she with Fox's inspiring sermons that the following Sunday, she approached him with an offer he couldn't refuse. She told him she was a stenographer and showed him shorthand notes she had taken of his sermon that Sunday. She offered to type them up, mimeograph them, and make them available to Fox's growing mailing list.

He readily agreed, and the thread was sewn. Aunt Hazel naturally put my mom (her sister) on the mailing list and soon Fox's sermons, fresh off the mimeo machine, began to arrive at our front door mail slot in Toronto.

My parents had been strict Canadian Anglican churchgoers but they had stopped going some time ago, saying the sermons were rote and boring. So when Fox's epistles came smoking through the mail slot, my mom was given her initial exposure to this "New Thought stuff." Almost immediately she and then my dad began to feel a shift in their lives. Worries and concerns about health and prosperity began to melt away. Stress about how to feed our growing family were dramatically exchanged for faith, trust, and confidence. This new thread began to weave and wend its way into the McClure household.

My mother began to check the newspapers and the Yellow Pages to see whether any New Thought churches were operating in Toronto. She finally found one near downtown. It was called (are you ready for this?) the Unity Church of Truth.

Later, she learned this was one of the 22 Churches of Truth that Dr. Albert Grier had formed as he traveled around the U.S. and Canada. In fact, the Toronto church was founded in 1914, one year after the Spokane ministry.

Within a few weeks, my parents decided to attend services there. They found out the church had a Sunday school, so they bundled up me and my two brothers to join them. I remember we had to take three buses to get there since we lived some distance from the church. We arrived to discover that the "church" was located on the third floor of an office building on a very busy street.

I can still remember climbing those wooden stairs, up and up and up, until we reached the top floor and entered a large room that during the week housed a ballet studio.

This church was under the leadership of a young, warm, and energetic couple who greeted us at the door and invited us in. Little did I know at the time, but I was about to enter the world of Unity, which I have never left. To say nothing of the woman minister who greeted us. Her name was Dorothy O'Connor. Later I was to know her as Dorothy Pierson, a matriarch and a legend in Unity.

The very first words I heard in a Unity church on that first Sunday were spoken by Dorothy as an opening invocation. And those words, which were to become my rallying cry and my ultimate affirmation were: "There is only One Presence and One Power in the Universe, God the Good, Omnipotent." Later I shortened this to OPOPGGO! And now, my name for God is, as you well know, the Unifying Thread or the other name I use from time to time—UFIP (Universal Field of Infinite Possibilities). Whatever name you have for God will work perfectly.

We loved our experience at the Toronto church so much that soon my parents were regular and enthusiastic members, and my brothers and I were regular Sunday school students.

I remember learning and memorizing a prayer on the very first Sunday. It was called "The Prayer of Faith" by Hannah More Kohaus. We began saying this prayer at bedtime—especially the last verse: "God is my health, I can't be sick; God is my strength, unfailing, quick; God is my all, I know no fear; Since God and Love and Truth are here."

I would use this prayer before taking a test at school or going to the doctor or the dentist. Little did I know this prayer would help save my life down the road.

Threads for Discussion

1. Where were you born?

2. What were your living conditions at an early age?

3. Did you have an uneventful childhood, or were there some unusual experiences that would follow you later into your life?

4. What was your early religious training, if any?

5. Is there any difference for you between belonging to a religion and following a spiritual path?

THE GUN AND THE CHICKADEE

Chapter 16

Pull a thread in my story and feel the tremor half a world and two millennia away.—Daniel Taylor

As I started to "thread" my way through my life experience, I recall an early incident that, now looking back, was one of the first signs there truly was a guiding and protecting Presence at work in my life, which to this day I am still trying to fully understand, grasp, and appreciate.

My dad loved to fish and hunt. Spending a lot of our lives in the country, he would, depending on the season, find himself and members of our family out on a boat fishing or in the woods hunting for deer or pheasant or partridge. As his three sons got older, we were encouraged to join him on these forays into the lakes, rivers, and brush of the Muskoka District where we lived.

One autumn, after my 12th birthday, my dad took me aside and said I was now old enough to hold a gun and I was ready to join him and my two older brothers out in the woods to hunt partridge. I remember being torn between wanting to please my father, wanting to join my two brothers for some "manly" adventure, and not being sure I wanted to shoot birds.

Somewhat reluctantly, I agreed to join the hunting party one fall morning. The party consisted of my dad, my older brother Don, and my brother Bob. We drove out into the country until we came to a wooded area that was far away from civilization. After exiting the car, my dad presented me with an instrument I had only seen in a locked cabinet in the garage—a gun. He said it was a single-shot, 12-gauge shotgun. He spent a considerable amount of time showing me how to load, carry, and shoot this weapon. He gave me three shotgun shells and loaded one into the chamber as we headed off into the bush.

After reaching what my dad called a good spot, he told us to spread out and head into the dense woods. He pointed to a wooded area on the right and said, "David, this will be your hunting territory. Go shoot us a partridge!"

As I began to walk through the trees and heavy underbrush, deeper into my area all by myself, I felt alone for probably the first time in my life. My mind was racing a mile a minute, both urging me on to look for, find, and shoot a partridge—I wasn't even sure what one looked like—while another part of me was saying, *David, you don't want to have any part of killing such a beautiful thing as this bird.* And so, with every step through the brush, I felt more and more certain that the last thing I wanted to do was to aim my gun at a poor, defenseless creature and blast it to smithereens.

But what would my dad say if I came out of the woods without even firing a shot and certainly with no prey that we would pluck, clean, and roast for dinner? And what would my brothers say? I would never live it down—the mocking, the joking, the kidding. These guys could be brutal at times.

My mind was ready to explode as I weighed the choices before me. I finally decided to sit down on a stump that caught my eye as I trudged through the underbrush.

Having sat, I thought. Without knowing what I was doing, I got quiet and went into my mind. Then I sat some more and thought some more. *What should I do? Should I join the ranks of the hunting McClures or chicken out and face the humiliation I was sure would come?*

Suddenly, things became very, very still. It was a quietness that I would discover often in my life ahead, but this was a first for me. I'll never forget it.

I was sitting on the stump with my gun across my lap when suddenly I was joined by one of God's most beautiful creations. A chickadee flew down from above and perched itself on the barrel of my 12-gauge shotgun. There I was, just sitting there minding my own business, deep in thought, and there was this bird on my gun, a bird that I immediately believed was there representing all the birds of the world.

As I gazed down at the little fellow, my way forward became crystal clear—I would never hunt with a gun again. I would never even carry a gun again. And I would never knowingly kill anything or anyone—ever. I would honor the life in all of God's creatures always.

As quickly as the chickadee appeared on my gun, it was gone, flying off to its next appointed task or errand but leaving me with a clear sense of direction (dare I say a *thread*) that would carry me through the rest of my life.

I was brought back to my senses by the sound of gunfire blasting to my left and to my right. Ah, some in my family had found their targets. I shuddered.

After meeting up with Dad, Don, and Bob, I could see they had all been successful in their hunt. They asked about my experience.

I told the truth, that I had not seen any partridge and took no shots. I did not tell them about my chickadee encounter. There was no chastising or criticism from anyone. All my dad said was, "Well, Davey, maybe next time!"

I knew in my heart of hearts there would never be a next time. And there never was.

I have now come to believe that this thing I call OPOPGGO had everything to do with my visit from the natural kingdom.

Threads for Discussion ──────────────────────────

1. Have you had encounters with the world of nature that have been memorable to you?

2. What did you learn from those encounters?

3. Do you believe a thread of some kind joins the natural world with your journey through life? How would you describe that thread?

THE SPOKANE THREAD
Chapter 17

Each of us has a purpose for living beyond our own survival and pleasure. Every individual is like a thread in a beautiful tapestry with a vital contribution to make, not only to the sustenance of life as we know it, but in the creation and development of more beneficial expressions of life.
—John Templeton

The Spokane thread, a strand of the guiding thread, first made its presence known to me in my teenage years. Fully entrenched in the Unity Church of Truth in Toronto, I continued through Sunday school and then to the teenage group called Youth of Unity or YOU.

Each year, YOU from all over North America and other parts of the world would gather at Unity Village, the headquarters of the Unity movement just outside Kansas City, Missouri. They would come together for the YOU Conference, a weeklong experience to meet with teens from all over who shared one common thread— Unity. There would be meetings, dances, fun and games, as well as spiritually oriented experiences led by the teens themselves.

I couldn't wait to attend one of these gatherings I had heard so much about. Finally, in 1951 when I was not quite 14, I was invited to join members of the Toronto chapter on an overnight bus ride from Toronto to Unity Village.

There were upward of 200 teens at the conference, and it turned out to be a blast. I got to serve on several committees and made some great new friends. I felt as though I was in my element, and I couldn't have been happier.

A cute blonde girl with a vivacious smile caught my eye. Her name was Sheri Stovin. But she caught every guy's eye as she made her way around the Unity grounds, always, it seemed, surrounded by teenage hunks. I was no match for these guys, so I kept a healthy distance. But there was something about Sheri that stuck with me while I was there at the conference, as well as when I returned home. I learned she was from a place called Spokane, Washington.

Threads for Discussion ─────────────────────────────

1. Have you ever met someone you had an interest in or a fascination with who showed up later in your life? How did that turn out?

2. What were some of your most memorable teenage experiences and relationships?

3. Do you still stay in touch with people you knew as teenagers?

4. What kind of person were you back in your teenage years?

"HERE AM I, LORD. USE ME."

Chapter 18

Then I heard the voice of the Lord saying, "Whom shall I send, and who will go for us?" And I said, "Here am I; send me!" —Isaiah 6:8

Early on, I knew my life would be about some form of communication. As a teenager, I worked a couple of summers in Port Sydney in the community hall. I did the announcing and emceed gigs for some events held there, played music for dances, and generally had a microphone in my hand at least once a week. Every year in Port Sydney there was a great fall festival called The Cavalcade of Color. I used to be the emcee for that occasion as well.

In high school, aside from being in the marching band, blowing my trumpet and beating my drum, I was in a few school plays and musicals and even gave a few speeches.

It was natural that I would choose radio and TV as my college major. I envisioned myself following in the footsteps and voice prints of famous news announcers—Lorne Greene in Toronto (who later starred in a TV show called *Bonanza*), and, of course, Walter Cronkite of CBS. I was blessed with an above-average speaking voice, so whatever I was going to end up doing with the rest of my life, my vocal cords would be prominently involved.

But even after winning a scholarship to Ryerson Technical Institute (now Toronto Metropolitan University) and landing a disc jockey gig on a local radio station in Toronto, I was to discover the broadcast media was a highly competitive, dog-eat-dog career. In my last year at Ryerson, I was still feeling uncertain and unsettled about what lay ahead.

Talking to my mother about my dilemma, she suggested I go have a talk with our current Unity minister. While most of the teens and early 20s kids whom I knew had stopped going to church for one reason or another—too uncool, too boring—I had held onto the thread of being part of Unity since my first encounter at age 7.

Taking my mother's advice, I made an appointment to see the woman who was then Unity minister at the Toronto church. She listened attentively as I told her my tale of having committed to a career in broadcasting but still feeling dissatisfied and unsure about who I was and what I was to become for the rest of my life.

After taking in my story, she looked deep into my eyes, smiled, and said, "David, I'm going to give you a short prayer to use to help you find your way and give you the guidance you're asking for. It's a prayer that I have used often and offered to many. But I must caution you, this is an extremely powerful prayer. It is powerful because it works. So, it comes with this warning label: *Do not use unless you really want your life to be transformed!* If you use it, it's going to change you. It will take over your life. So what do you choose? Do you want me to give you this prayer?"

"Oh, yes! I am ready! Please share it with me! What is this prayer?"

She said (and here's my intro to the guiding thread), "Here am I, Lord. Use me!"

"That's it?" I asked.

"That's it!" she said.

I don't know what I was expecting, but probably something bigger than a simple affirmation. I thanked her and went home with the prayer of prayers in my mind and soon to be on my lips.

Since it was late in the day when I got home, I decided to save the prayer until I was bright and perky in the morning. My usual deep sleep was interrupted a few times as the prayer kept creeping in and wrapping itself around my conscious mind. Finally, I told myself to let go and let God, and fell deeply asleep.

I awakened early the next morning before the sun was up. There, in the privacy of my bedroom, I spoke the words: "Here am I, Lord. Use me!"

I waited for something to happen, but nothing did. I spoke it two more times, just to be sure I'd given it my whole attention. I finished with a rousing "Thank you!" Then I got dressed and ate breakfast. My mom asked me how my session with the Unity minister had gone. I said, "Oh, fine" and left it at that. I kissed her goodbye and headed off to class.

The classes that day were uneventful. The last class of the day was English literature. I sat there completely bored, wishing I could be somewhere else. I cannot tell you what the professor was covering that day, and I didn't really care. I found myself staring out the window at the passing scene.

And then I heard The Voice.

It was the clearest, calmest, most concise voice I have ever heard. I looked around the room but immediately knew it wasn't coming from a human being there in the classroom. It was a voice coming from within me. And it came with all power and clarity of one speaking with authority, one with firsthand knowledge, and above all, one with love. The Voice said: "David, you are going to be a Unity minister. This is to be your path."

I sat up straight in my chair and tried to absorb what I had just heard. I found no argument in me, no resistance, and, to my surprise, no defense.

I left school that day and hurried home to tell my mom about The Voice. I told her in the clearest terms possible. I said, "Mom, yesterday, the Unity minister gave me a prayer to use. She told me that it came with a warning label."

"Warning label?" she questioned.

"Yeah. The warning label was about not using this prayer unless you really want results because it really works. Don't use it unless you really want your life to be transformed. So this morning, I decided I wanted my life to change. So I used the prayer."

"What was the prayer?" she inquired.

"The prayer was 'Here am I, Lord. Use me.'"

"So did it work?"

"Well, I think it did. Today in class I heard a voice like no voice I had ever heard before. It was coming from deep within me. It was as clear as anything I have ever heard."

My mom smiled and looked into my eyes. "And what did the voice say to you, David?"

"The Voice said that I am going to be a Unity minister and that this was my path."

There wasn't a change in her expression one bit. She laughed and replied, "Well, I could have told you that, David! I've always known that to be your true calling."

"You did? Then why didn't you ever tell me that?" I challenged.

"Because that's something you must discover for yourself. No one else can do that for you."

Stunned by the certainty of her gaze, her voice, and her smile, it was as though, at some point in her life, perhaps even before I was born, she had received strands of the guiding thread telling of my spiritual destiny and she had been keeping these close to her heart until I took hold of them myself.

We talked for what seemed like hours, until my dad, my two brothers, and my younger sister came home, and I relayed my story about The Voice. While they lacked the certainty of my mother's intuitive knowing, they all seemed to celebrate the good news that I finally knew what I was going to do when I grew up.

We talked about it over dinner. Weary and overwhelmed by the day's event, I went to bed early. I remember my mom coming into my bedroom and saying to me, before I drifted off, "David, if you want a little more certainty about this guidance that you received today, why not make another appointment with our Unity minister and see what she has to say?"

I agreed this was a great idea and called her the next day to set up another appointment.

Entering her office, I immediately felt her love and support. I felt so at ease in her presence. I told her I had used the prayer she gave me and that, within six hours of speaking it, I heard this clear, powerful, convincing voice within me declaring, with all certainty, as though I was talking to the God of the Universe, that my path through this lifetime was going to be that of a Unity minister.

The smile on her face at hearing this news was very close to the smile my mother had displayed the day before when I gave her the news. Not only that, but the words that came out of her mouth were the same as my mom's. "Well, David, really! I've always known that about you. You can't be anything else, but you had to hear it straight from the horse's mouth!"

And so, my course was set. I'm glad my mother and my minister knew what my life was to be about. I guess I wouldn't know until I was good and ready and willing to listen. I now know that this

Voice was the guiding thread speaking through my mind. This thread had now surfaced and would lead me toward some kind of great spiritual adventure—the adventure that I still find myself living today, even as I write these words.

The unifying threads that have kept showing up in my life are the threads of heart (feeling) and mind (thinking). I have likened them to my human heroes—Myrtle (heart) and Charles (mind) Fillmore. I now believe these threads have been showing up and revealing themselves to any heart and mind willing to listen since at least the beginning of life on this planet. These are the threads mentioned in Genesis as the masculine and feminine. "Then God said, 'Let us make humans in our image, according to our likeness ...' So God created humans in his image, in the image of God he created them; male and female he created them" (Genesis 1:26, 27).

And so, as I began to find my spiritual roots, I discovered my inner guidance system, which was to lead me to what I was destined to be.

Threads for Discussion ────────────────────────

1. Have others known things about your destiny before you did? What sorts of things did they know?

2. Did any of those things eventually shape the rest of your life? Where did they take you and when did they show up?

3. Are you living out your true destiny right now, or do you think there are unfinished pieces still waiting to be revealed?

4. Is surrender a key element when we are seeking healing or guidance? Is letting go and letting God important in order to receive guidance, healing, or results?

"WHAT MAKES YOU THINK
YOU CAN BE A UNITY MINISTER?"

Chapter 19

*And the faith that grows out of questioning is
stronger than the faith born of blind acceptance.*
—James Dillet Freeman

As I continued to follow the guiding thread that had been
dramatically laid out before me, I applied to the ministerial
program at Unity School of Christianity at Unity Village in
Missouri. After finishing my college adventure in 1959 with decent
results, I knew all the training in broadcast radio and television
would prove to be an asset as I traveled along the path of ministry
before me.

As mentioned earlier in this book, I visited the magnificent
grounds of Unity Village in my early teen years as a member of the
Toronto Youth of Unity. I knew the thread that was now drawing
me back was one that I had started experiencing in church at the
age of 7 and had continued throughout my teenage years. I knew
there was magic in this place. I could feel the presence of Myrtle
and Charles Fillmore there.

I nervously awaited a reply to my application. Finally, a letter
showed up in our Toronto mailbox. I remember being alone
that day when the mailman came, and I watched him drop some
envelopes through the mail slot. I scrambled to the door and
glanced down at six or seven envelopes lying on the floor. Then I
spotted it.

I could make out the return address on one of the envelopes—
Unity School of Christianity, Lee's Summit, Missouri. As I reached
down to grab it, I could feel my heart pumping. I tore open the
envelope and removed the letter from inside. A new thread was
about to become my future.

This is what I read: "We have received your application and
would love to talk with you about the Unity Ministerial Program.
The director of the Ministerial Program, Rev. James Dillet Freeman,

would like to meet with you within the next month to determine whether you are qualified to be a Unity minister. Please call the school to make an appointment."

I knew of Jim Freeman. I had been inspired by his poetry in *Daily Word* magazine, his articles in *Unity Magazine*, and some of his early books, such as *The Household of Faith*, *The Story of Unity*, and my favorite, a collection of poems he had simply titled *Be!* He would go on to write a dozen or so other books.

Freeman was sometimes referred to as the poet laureate of Unity and later as the poet laureate to the moon because his poems were twice carried by astronauts to the moon, a distinction he shares with no other author. His "Prayer for Protection" was taken aboard Apollo 11 in July 1969 by Edwin "Buzz" Aldrin, who followed Neil Armstrong down the ladder of the Eagle module onto the moon. Then a microfilm of Freeman's poem "I Am There" was left on the moon by Jim Irwin on Apollo 15. I was eager to meet Freeman, who was already a legendary figure in the Unity movement and beyond. I was later to know him as a soul who inspired and influenced my life and my ministry more than anyone else.

I waited for my parents to arrive home to give them the good news. Of course, they were overjoyed, and I could see the wheels turning in their minds as they began planning for my departure to Missouri for my interview.

Eventually the day came for my journey south. It was a late summer day in 1959 when I boarded a bus in Toronto that would take me to Rochester, New York (the hometown of my mother and her family, including the amazing Aunt Hazel). There I changed buses for the overnight journey to Kansas City.

Weary and somewhat disoriented, I arrived at the Kansas City bus station where I was met by a very kind woman who drove me the final 15 miles or so to the hallowed grounds of Unity Village. As we approached our destination, I kept my eye out for the historic landmark that would say we were "home"—Unity Tower. The tower was completed in 1929 to provide 100,000 gallons of potable water storage for the Unity School of Christianity campus. The

165-foot tower, also a bell tower or *campanile* built in a modified Italian Renaissance style, can be seen for miles around.

Upon arrival, I checked in at the motel there on the campus and settled myself in for what was to be, I thought, the most exciting day of my life, when I would finally meet the one, the only, the highly anticipated James Dillet Freeman.

After a somewhat restless sleep, I awoke and reiterated my special prayer. "Here am I, Lord. Use me!" After breakfast at the Unity Inn, I found what was then the Silent Unity Building and Rev. Freeman's office. His office, I was to find out later, had been previously occupied by none other than Charles Fillmore. Myrtle's office was just across the hall.

I could feel the guiding thread strong, sure, and daunting.

Freeman's secretary warmly greeted me and ushered me into his office. Once in, I looked across the office to find a man at the window, looking out at the fountains and magnificent rose garden that were and still are a central focus of the campus. He heard me come in but did not turn to face me.

Finally, he turned, and with eyes bluer than I had ever seen, looked me square in the face and asked me a question that I had not, in my wildest dreams, expected to be his first words to me. He said, "McClure, what makes you think you can be a Unity minister?"

To this day, I do not remember how I answered his challenging question. I think I said something about praying my special prayer and hearing a voice that told me this was what my life was going to be. I told him about Aunt Hazel transcribing Emmet Fox's sermons and my parents finding Unity in Toronto. I told him of being in Unity Sunday school and then in YOU and attending some conferences at the Village in my teen years. I think I told him that I loved his writings and was honored to be talking to him face-to-face.

I remember he asked me some other questions, but I can't tell you what they were except for one—he asked my age. I told him I was 22.

Finally, he looked at me with his penetrating blue eyes, smiled, and said, "Dave, I recommend that you go back home to Toronto and get a little more experience in living and working under your belt. Then come back and see me, and we'll see if you have what it takes to become a Unity minister."

My heart dropped. I thought I was a shoo-in for the ministry and now he was telling me I was still wet behind the ears and needed to bulk up on work and living experience. What a bummer! I thanked him, we shook hands, and I headed out of his office with my tail between my legs and a deep frown on my face.

Returning to Toronto, I sadly gave my parents the news and wondered what I would do next. I remember my mom saying, "This is perfect, David. Just think, soon you'll be all you need to be to fulfill your calling."

My thread seemed a bit frayed right then, but it was not broken; it just had a kink in it.

The thread now led me to my brother Donald. At the time, he was a journalist for a local newspaper called *The Northern Miner*. He said he would see whether there were any job openings at his paper and sure enough there was one. It was working in the addressograph department, which back in those days created the type on metal plates that were then used to print out mailing labels for addressing the hundreds of newspapers to subscribers.

At first, I thought this was going to be a boring and mundane kind of job with nothing to enhance my résumé for the ministry. I was so wrong. It turned out to be as enriching and fulfilling an experience as I had ever had at that point in my life.

In the ministerial program, typing would be an essential skill. Mr. Freeman had told me part of the ministerial training consisted of working in the letter writing department of Silent Unity, the prayer ministry originally founded by the Fillmores and the heart of the Unity mission. Back then, before computers and cell phones, the fastest way people could communicate was with a typewriter. It hadn't really registered with me when he mentioned it, but now it was crystal clear.

And so, I spent the better part of a year working, typing, and maturing in every way I could.

The next year, 1960, I once again made the bus journey south to Unity. Once again, I was met at the bus station and once again took that ride past the Unity Tower and into Unity Village. Again, after a good night's sleep and breakfast, I was in the office of The Man.

This time, he rushed to greet me, shook my hand, and smiled openly. He had read through my report on the additional elements of the year that was now behind me. After a few more questions, and apparently the right answers, he told me he would love to welcome me into the Unity Ministerial Training Program. He told me to make plans to come to the Village to live, work, and study.

I did. And two years later, I became a licensed Unity minister.

The guiding thread continued.

Threads for Discussion —————————————————————————

1. Have you ever heard a voice inside of you directing you to a new career or another direction for your life? What did this voice say to you?

2. Did you follow the guidance from this voice? If you did, where did it lead you? If you didn't, why not?

3. If you did follow your guidance, were there obstacles that showed up along the way? Did they delay, stop, or discourage you?

4. Is your life today the result of following your voice?

AS SACRED AS THE BISON

Chapter 20

From the animist point of view, humans belong in a sacred place because they themselves are sacred. Not sacred in a special way, not more sacred than anything else, but merely as sacred as anything else—as sacred as bison or salmon or crows or crickets or bears or sunflowers.—Daniel Quinn

I completed ministerial training and became a licensed Unity minister in 1962. Although I didn't quite feel ready, according to Unity School I was trustworthy enough to go into what was called The Field to begin ministering to a real live Unity congregation.

Within a month or two of my graduation, I was called into Jim Freeman's office. He had a wide smile on his face. He sat me down and asked me a couple of simple questions: "McClure, you're from Canada, right? Are you still a Canadian citizen?"

I answered in the affirmative to both questions.

He said, "Good! We have a request from the Unity Church in Vancouver, British Columbia, for an associate minister. Would you be interested in going there?"

My heart just about leaped out of my chest. "Sure," I said. "I've always wanted to see the Northwest, and the opportunity to be back in Canada would be fantastic!"

"Good!" said Freeman. "Pack your bags. You don't even have to try out there. They have read your credentials, and I've told them what great ministerial potential you have, so they decided to take my word for it." To receive that kind of endorsement from a Unity legend lifted my spirits to new heights.

So pack I did, stuffing everything I owned in the trunk and back seat of my 1957 Ford Fairlane 500.

I hadn't realized how hard it would be to leave this place that had been my spiritual home base for two years. Besides all the great memories and feelings living in me, there were friends, colleagues, and even a girlfriend, who, sadly, I had to hug, kiss, and bid a fond farewell.

But with my girlfriend tearfully waving as I drove out the gates of Unity Village, I headed north to the new adventure that was ahead. I knew I would return to the Village many times in the ensuing years. One return was a sure thing—I would be back for my ordination in one year!

I had mapped out my route from Missouri to British Columbia ahead of time. I arrived just south of Flagstaff, Arizona, early one morning. I was merrily driving up a very steep incline on a totally vacant stretch of highway when I began to feel that I was no longer being propelled forward. I sensed that possibly my transmission was about to give out on me. I prayed I would have enough momentum to reach the top of the hill.

You can imagine what my first thoughts were. *Not now, baby girl!* (My car was female, I believed. Her name was Rhonda. Don't ask me why.) A million thoughts were swirling through my head, and my heart was pounding down on the floorboards somewhere. *What if this is the end of my car and the end of my journey? Here I am way out in the boonies. There's no traffic at this time of the day. I haven't spotted another car for miles. And there certainly can't be any gas stations out here in no-man's-land.*

But then, a voice, actually the guiding thread inside me, chimed in and said those sweet, beautiful words that I have used a million times, *David, divine order! Don't you remember that I always have and will always have your back?*

I urged Rhonda onward, coaxing her to take me at least to the top of this hill so I could coast down the other side to whatever was down there. She was not giving up and thankfully, mercifully, we reached the top of the hill. I had no transmission at all. Now all I had was gravity.

I looked down on the highway below me in the dim light of morning. At first all I saw was a vast and barren stretch of empty roadway ahead of me. After all, I was in the middle of the desert. Then my eye caught something in the far distance. Was that a light shining into the dawn? Yes, I saw a single, solitary light.

Even though I had no transmission, I shifted the gear into neutral. I let Rhonda coast down the hill and down we went. I reckoned the hill was about five miles long. As we got closer to the light, I made out a Route 66 sign shining brightly before my very eyes.

Oh, dear guiding thread, yes! It was a sight for sore eyes. A service station! As I leveled off at the foot of the hill, I had just enough oomph to coast into the station with the most magnificent sign I had ever seen: Open 24 Hours.

I went into the office and told the friendly guy how thankful I was to see him and asked him if he was a mirage in the desert or was this a real, genuine service station. He assured me this was about as real as service stations get. I explained to him my transmission had quit, and I just made it to the top of the hill and coasted down the other side. I told him I was headed to British Columbia to take on a new job there. I asked him if he had any solutions.

He said, "The best I can do is call you a tow truck to come out here, pick you and your car up, and take you back to Flagstaff."

I thanked him for his solution and sat myself down with a nice, hot cup of coffee and a packet of Twinkies.

About an hour later, a tow truck arrived. I was never so happy to see a tow truck in my life. The logo on the side of the truck said Happy's Towing Service. I smiled to myself and murmured under my breath, "You've got that right!" I went out and greeted the driver. I explained the problem to him. He said he was willing to tow me back to Flagstaff (about 20 miles) for $100. My funds were limited at the time, but I had no choice but to accept his offer.

He hitched up Rhonda, I climbed into the passenger side of the truck, and off we went, back up the road I had just maneuvered down.

Eventually we arrived at an auto repair shop, where the driver unloaded both me and my car. I paid him the $100, thanked him, and headed into the office of the auto shop and told the guy behind the desk my sad story.

I will always remember how friendly and cheerful this guy was. In fact, all the men I had encountered that morning—the gas station attendant, the tow truck operator, and now this guy—

were all especially warm, congenial, and helpful on this day. I remember thinking at the time that divine order was going the extra mile for me and I had been visited by a band of auto angels sent to me directly from the guiding thread.

The mechanic came out, opened Rhonda's hood, and then buried himself under the hood. He then closed the hood and slid under the car. After a few minutes, he came up for air and announced that it definitely was a transmission problem. He said he would have to order parts to fix this, and it would take a couple of days.

Hmm. A couple of days.

Well, there was nothing I could do but find myself a motel and settle into Flagstaff and wait this out. Another divine order was a motel within walking distance of the repair shop. I opened Rhonda's trunk and took out my overnight bag, secured the rest of my belongings, patted the car on the fender, and headed over to the motel.

For the next two days and nights, I did a little looking around downtown Flagstaff, and on the third morning, I was pleased to hear that my car was ready to rock 'n' roll. The bill was another $150. My savings were slowly dwindling.

But, now happy to be on my way, I thanked the repairman and once again headed west. Still having some time on my hands before I was scheduled to be in Vancouver, I decided to take a swing through Las Vegas, just to say I had seen The Strip. And then on through Utah and then north to Wyoming. I had a very important reason for seeing Wyoming.

Wyoming was going to take me through *buffalo country*! I had never seen an American bison, but something within me had always been fascinated whenever I saw pictures, read articles, or watched movies about these amazing creatures.

"Oh, please, guiding thread," I prayed, "please let me see at least one buffalo!"

I reached Wyoming in the late afternoon. There were plenty of wide-open spaces where buffalo might roam, but as I kept one eye on the road and the other on the grassy plains that spread out for miles on either side of the car, I spotted nothing that even resembled the beast.

As I drove on, I realized I would soon be out of Wyoming and my chances of seeing a real live, genuine American bison were fading. It was going on 6 p.m. when, weary and hungry, I decided to look for a place to take a break and eat the sandwich I had purchased in Flagstaff. Up ahead, I found a small picnic area on my side of the road, so I pulled over and parked.

There was but one picnic table, which was down a slope beside a sparkling, running stream. By this time, not only was I tired, not only was I hungry, but I was feeling very alone and disoriented.

I took out the sandwich and the cola that came with it and sat down at the picnic table facing the creek. I sighed a lot, ate some, and looked at the water occasionally. Here I was, out in the middle of nowhere, with nothing but Rhonda to keep me company, headed for a job I knew nothing about. I don't know when I had felt so lonely and out of touch. Even with the flowing stream of life right there in front of me, I found myself yearning for some company—some reassurance, some sign.

Just as I was about to be a grown man who cries, I heard a sound behind me. It was a very loud *snort*. It scared the daylights out of me. And then there was another *snort*.

Slowly, I turned around to see what I had been hoping, wishing, and praying to see for years now standing not more than 50 yards away. I was looking at a single, huge, hairy, magnificent creature that I immediately recognized as you-know-what!

My heart was in my throat. My emotions at that moment were mixed between elation and sheer terror. I had heard that folks at Yellowstone had been attacked and gored by these animals. Goring was not on my prayer list that day. But buffaloes most certainly were.

My terror thoughts finally won the battle. Slowly, I put my sandwich down and climbed up to the top of the picnic table. There began a staring match between the big boy over there and the little boy atop the table. I noticed my knees were shaking.

After a period of time I cannot measure, as we stared at each other, something otherworldly happened. I began to feel a slight vibration in the table I was standing on. This tremor slowly began to escalate as I stood there. Pretty soon, I thought the shaking was going to knock me off the table and onto the ground.

And then I saw them. Over a rise in the woods beside me came one, two, three, and then 50 of the biggest, shaggiest, most beautiful beasts I have ever seen.

They walked slowly and deliberately over the hill, taking no heed of me. The solo lookout guy who had initially appeared broke off from me and joined the herd, and they marched not more than 10 feet past me down to the stream, where they commenced to refresh themselves in the sparkling water.

I watched them from atop the table for as long as the fading sunlight would allow. Then reluctantly but wisely, I stepped down from the table, grabbed my sandwich, and made it back to the car.

My prayer had been answered and then some. Thank you, guiding thread!

Threads for Discussion

1. Have you ever had an answer to prayer that went beyond your wildest dreams? What was the prayer and what was the answer?

2. Have you ever been in a situation where you were both scared and excited at the same time? What kind of situation was this?

3. Have your own answers to prayer been sufficient over the years to build a strong faith and trust in OPOPGGO (One Presence and One Power, God the Good, Omnipotent)?

4. Have you ever had any encounters with buffalo? If so, what was your experience and how did you feel about it?

"GO GET 'EM, TIGER!"

Chapter 21

The events in our lives happen in a sequence in time, but in their significance to ourselves they find their own order ... the continuous thread of revelation. — Eudora Welty

Buoyed by my brief but beautiful buffalo encounter, I finally came to the border crossing into Canada. Being a Canadian citizen at the time, I had little trouble immigrating back into "the True North strong and free."

I headed farther north, finally reaching my destination— the beautiful, and I mean *beautiful*, city of Vancouver, British Columbia. It's got to be one of the most picturesque and scenic cities in the world. I could hardly wait to get settled and begin exploring this magnificent city by the Pacific Ocean.

People at the Unity ministry there had found me a small apartment with rent well within the salary I had been offered. It was on the third floor of a well-maintained mansion, not far from the "church."

I write the word "church" in quotation marks because Unity Church of Vancouver did not have a church building at that time. Its offices were in a building called the Scottish Auditorium, which they rented from the Gaelic Society of Vancouver. Having Scottish ancestry in my blood (another thread), I knew I would be happy amongst the Scots. Sunday services for Unity were held in the old Stanley Movie Theatre on Granville Street.

On my first day in the office, I met the senior minister, who seemed like a very likable chap. He greeted me warmly and welcomed me to my very first job as a Unity minister. He spent an hour or so telling me about the ministry in Vancouver then ushered me into my tiny office, which already had a sign on the door—David McClure, Assistant Minister.

What a rush! To see my name on a ministerial door. The threads were further connecting with and for me.

I settled in and got to work on what assistant ministers are supposed to do, which was mainly to take and make phone calls, make hospital visits, and open the mail.

When Sunday arrived, I arrived early at the theater (spelled *theatre* in Canada). Every day but Sunday, this was a busy movie house with first-run films drawing audiences that filled the 600 or so seats in the auditorium. As I arrived, I found the volunteer church ushers scurrying about, doing whatever ushers do before there's anyone to usher.

The senior minister welcomed me and showed me around. He introduced me to his wife then took me to meet the bookstore manager, an attractive blonde who was opening boxes she had brought over from the Scottish Auditorium and was busily putting out books that would be offered for sale to the congregation. Her "bookstore" was the popcorn stand in the theater lobby.

I met all the staff and volunteers ahead of the service, then the congregation began to pour in. I was astounded to see that as the 11 a.m. hour approached, most of the 600 seats were filled.

The senior minister told me to sit in the front row, and as the service progressed, he finally introduced me and called me forward. There was a round of polite applause as I walked up the steps on stage right and joined him at the podium. I said a few words about being so glad to be back in Canada and especially about the beauty of their city. I felt truly honored and blessed to be a part of their Unity family.

And so, my ministerial career was off and running. Things went smoothly for several months. I was given more responsibility and even got to lead meditations on Sundays occasionally.

And then, on a particular Sunday, everything changed.

I arrived as usual to perform the duties I had been instructed to do. The enthusiastic crowd began to arrive, and at 10 minutes to 11 a.m., one of the ushers came to me and said, "David, the senior minister called me before I left home and conveyed to me that he and the bookstore manager would not be coming in this morning. In fact, the senior minister said that he and the bookstore manager would *never* be coming back to the Stanley

Theatre ever again, because they were leaving town and would not be returning—ever!" He waited to catch his breath and then continued. "Well, David, it looks like you're it. Right now, you're all we've got."

A wave of panic shot through me. I muttered a reaction that was something to the effect of, "You're joking, right? You've got to be joking!"

To which he replied, "I wish I were, but that's just the way it is. So get ready, you're on in 10 minutes."

My heart was in my socks by then. What would I do? What would I say? How would the congregation take the news that their very own sweet and beloved minister had run off with the bookstore manager? I knew I couldn't tell them that last part, but what could I tell them?

I found the nearest bathroom and tried to keep from throwing up. I put cold water on my face and tried to gather my composure. And while I was doing these things, a voice deep within said, *David, what is that prayer that was given to you before you knew you were going to be a Unity minister?*

Oh, that prayer. *"Here am I, Lord. Use me." Is that the one you mean?*

With no time to wait for an answer, I took a deep breath or three and uttered what had become for me the prayer of prayers.

"Here am I, Lord. Use me!"

Without checking to see whether I was calm or not, I left the restroom and made my way to the aisle at the back of the theater that would lead me to the stairs at stage right, where I would try to make it onstage without tripping, stumbling, throwing up, or quickly running out the side exit door.

The setup for Sundays had an usher stationed at each stairway to the stage. This was so they could escort folks up to the stage and detain people who might feel it necessary to barge up the stairs and attack the speaker or, more likely, say a few words themselves.

As I approached the stairs, there stood a very tall, handsome man whom I had come to know as George. He knew what I now knew, and he knew that I was the one designated to share the wild and crazy story of what was going on with our senior minister and the bookstore manager.

As I passed him, he smiled. Then he reached out and punched me in the arm and said words I will never forget: "Go get 'em, Tiger!"

It was as though a bolt of lightning shot through me. I felt invigorated, confident, and clear. I marched up on the stage to face the music.

Threads for Discussion

1. Have you ever been put in an emergency where you've had to ad-lib your way to some semblance of order? How did that turn out?

2. What qualities did you discover within you that helped support you during this challenge?

3. Did you have time to pray about this situation ahead of time? If so, what was your prayer?

4. How are you when you're put on the spot to step up and "save the day"?

THE THREAD LEADS ME DOWN UNDER

Chapter 22

*We make our way through everything like thread
passing through fabric, giving shape to images that
we ourselves do not know.*—Rainer Maria Rilke

Sometimes the guiding thread that weaves its way through our lives takes us in directions we never dreamed possible. There is no place on planet Earth, or perhaps beyond, where a healing or guiding thread of yours and mine cannot be found, nor do we know when we might connect or reconnect along our spiritual journey.

One evening after a class I was teaching at the Scottish Auditorium, a group of four young women approached me. They invited me to join them for coffee at a nearby hangout. Without hesitating, I said, "Sure!"

As we sat around a table at the coffee shop, they began to relate to me their *real* reason for inviting me that evening. They told me that the four of them had formed a small group called The Australia or Bust Group.

It was their plan and wish to move to Australia. In their reading and in their hearts, they had become fascinated with the country, its people, and the idea of adventure in a far-off land. They wanted to know if I would be their leader and help them achieve their dream.

I graciously thanked them for their invitation but said I didn't feel led to travel that far right then. My ministerial future was uncertain at the time. I didn't know how much longer I would be in Vancouver after the new senior minister arrived. And I didn't know what my status would be once he/she took the reins at Unity of Vancouver.

Sadly, they accepted my explanation, but as a parting gift they left me with a recent edition of the *Sydney Morning Herald*, hoping it might trigger the "Aussie" in me.

I thanked them and went back to my flat.

The next morning, out of curiosity, I decided to glance through the newspaper to see what Sydney had to offer. I don't know why or how, but I eventually found my way to the want ads and glanced over the personals printed therein. Suddenly, an ad caught my eye that was about to change my life.

It was an ad from, of all things, a Unity study group in Sydney, announcing its next Sunday service and welcoming newcomers to join. It gave an address for meetings plus a post office box address.

Wow! I thought. I sure didn't think there were Unity students attending Unity churches and centers that far away. I began to wonder who these folks were, how they had found one another, and how their group was faring.

I decided to write them a cheery greeting letter, letting them know I'd seen their ad in the *SMH* and just wanted to reach out to them. A few days later, I dropped my letter in a mailbox and got back to my Vancouver ministerial duties.

As the days passed, the gentleman who was to become the new senior minister for Unity of Vancouver arrived. He was a tall Texan with a drawl and a quick, friendly smile that was engaging. I knew he was the right and perfect Unity minister to lead these folks to places of greater glory and success than they had ever known.

I knew too that it was time for me to think about where I would be going next in the early stages of my ministerial career. I contacted Unity HQ, but they didn't have any openings at that time.

One evening, as I came home from the Scottish Auditorium office, I picked up my mail from the box in the lobby of my apartment building. As usual it was mostly junk mail, but then my eye caught a light blue envelope marked "air mail." It had several colorful stamps I did not recognize, but it was addressed to me. The return address indicated it was from the Unity group in Sydney.

My first thought was, *Oh, how sweet. They're writing a chummy note back to me, giving me a little more information about their small ministry and a wee bit of a warm, friendly greeting.*

Reaching my apartment and sinking into my one easy chair, I opened the letter.

I could not believe what I read. It has now been more than 50 years since this event, but as near as I can remember, the letter, neatly typed and brief, said, in effect: "Greetings, Rev. David. We are a small group of about 35 Unity students who meet in an office building at Circular Quay in Sydney. We are so thrilled to contact you! When can you come here to be our leader?"

I almost fell off my chair. This message could just as easily have come from another planet. Their words were direct, straightforward, and audacious. *"When can you come here to be our leader?"*

Moi? They want me to come from my home here in Canada and go all the way to the other side of the planet? Here before me was an open and loving invitation that went far beyond anything I could ever imagine. Was this worth praying about? Was it worth seriously considering? I decided it was. So, pray I did. And consider it I also did. *Here am I, Lord. Use me.* was once again front and center in my consciousness.

My guidance was to call Unity World Headquarters and get their viewpoint on such an undertaking. I was directed to the office of Rev. J. Sig Paulson, who at the time was director of the Department of World Unity. He was responsible for the growing number of Unity ministries that were developing in other countries.

In our conversation, Rev. Paulson became very excited and enthusiastic about the possibility of opening Unity centers in Australia. "And while you're down there," he said, "you could check out New Zealand as well."

I told him I didn't have the financial means to take such a long trip. He said he would investigate ways that World Unity could support me monetarily and would get back to me with more details soon.

As I hung up the phone, I began to wonder what it would be like living and working in a place I had only read about. More prayer time ensued, then even more.

A week later, Sig Paulson called me back and was pleased to tell me that World Unity would be able to award me a stipend of $500 a month. Further, he said that with the limited funds available for such an adventure, there would be money for my trip to Australia only if I went by sea and not by air.

Then he asked me, "David, is this a go?"

Somewhere from a place deep within me, a voice said, *David, go!*

I relayed the message to Sig, and the die was cast for me to head out on what would be one of the greatest adventures of my life. At my last Sunday service in Vancouver, I shared the news of my newest Unity ministry in of all places—Sydney, Australia! After the service, I met with my friends from the Australia or Bust Group. There were tears and, to my surprise, regrets since none of the four had openings in their lives right then to make the journey for themselves. But they were glad they had played a part in helping to make my journey happen.

Making it happen meant finding ocean travel from British Columbia to Australia. In the end, all I could find and all I could afford was a freighter that was leaving from Vancouver Island for Sydney in a few days. I felt a little embarrassed to tell my Vancouver friends that, despite a few passenger ships making the journey, all I could afford was this little, aging, somewhat rickety freighter.

Having said all my goodbyes and thanking everyone for their support through my ordeal in the Vancouver ministry, I packed a large steamer trunk with all my worldly belongings and made ready for the voyage.

On the day of departure, I boarded a bus in Vancouver, which then boarded a ferry, which eventually took me and my steamer trunk to a little town on Vancouver Island called Chemainus.

Chemainus is a community on the east coast of southern Vancouver Island. Today, this little town is a popular site for tourists, but in 1963, when I was being let off at the dock, it was famous for its large sawmill and little else. The name Chemainus comes from the native shaman and prophet *Tsa-meeun-is*, meaning "broken chest." Legend has it that a man survived a massive wound in his chest from an arrow in battle and went on to become a powerful chief.

So this was to be a place of overcoming, of healing, and now a place where a new thread in my life was about to unfurl.

Waiting at the dock was the ship scheduled to take me 8,000 miles across the Pacific Ocean to my next ministerial assignment. The ship was named the *SS Lakemba*. Built in 1945 in North Vancouver, she began her sailing adventure as a maintenance ship with the Royal Navy. She had been refitted to accommodate passengers and placed on a run that included Vancouver, Honolulu, American Samoa, Fiji, and Sydney.

Watching as my steamer trunk was taken off the bus and placed on board the ship, I found the gangplank and climbed to the passenger deck of what was to be my home for the next seven and a half weeks. I learned that freighters value cargo more than passengers, so they would be in no hurry to get to their final destination. I watched as lumber, cars, and various other pieces of cargo were loaded into the hold of the ship, overflowing now onto the decks, both fore and aft. I remember thinking to myself, *Not much room for what I hoped would be evening strolls on the deck.*

I was greeted by a friendly chap who welcomed me and ushered me to my cabin. My room was on that very same passenger deck not far from the ship's railing, which of course meant that it would be very, very close to the Pacific Ocean.

In the small cabin to which I had been assigned, I found the gentleman who would be my roommate for the voyage. He was jovial and talkative. The cabin was tiny. He pointed to the top bunk and said it would be mine. Since he had arrived first, he had claimed the bottom bunk. There was a small bathroom, a table, two chairs, and a dresser.

I was told to empty my clothes out of my trunk and then close it and lock it with the understanding it would be removed and put into storage below deck in the ship's hold.

Having accomplished all these housekeeping tasks, I stepped out on deck to survey the scene. Soon I heard what would become a familiar sound to me—the ship's horn. It seemed our ship was ready to depart before we were. The horn startled me and I felt my heart begin to pound.

I need to remind you that all of this was a totally new experience for me. It was my first time on a ship, my first time in the Pacific

Ocean or any ocean for that matter. And it was my first time to be this far from home. For a moment, I felt the same utter loneliness I had felt before encountering my first buffalo in Wyoming. I felt so helpless, so out of control. I had to remind myself that I was here courtesy of my very own guiding thread.

Soon I heard the ship's horn again and began to feel the engines turn below me. I watched from the railing as the lines were freed from the dock and the ship slipped from its moorings and slowly began to head out of the harbor toward the open sea.

I remember noting that there was no crowd waving goodbye as we gently began to move. In fact, there was only one, solitary soul watching from the dock. He appeared to be a Native Canadian man who wasn't waving goodbye but simply staring at us as we departed. That made me feel even lonelier than before.

As we made it through channels to the open sea, we were called to the mess hall for dinner and further instructions. Arriving there, I met the rest of my fellow passengers—almost 50 of us, I guess. I found nearly all these folks were as excited and nervous as I was about the voyage we would take across the Pacific. There were picnic tables for the diners, so I found a seat and started eating a wholesome meal and making new friends.

Weary after the long trip from Vancouver, I climbed up to my bunk early for what I hoped would be a good night's sleep with only a gentle rocking of the ship, which I soon adjusted to, and quickly dropped off into slumber.

Sometime in the middle of the night, I was awakened by shaking, rattling, and rolling like I had never experienced in my entire life. My roommate in the bunk below was swearing and cursing and informed me that we were in the middle of a typhoon.

I remember thinking about jumping out of the top bunk, but instead I ended up falling out. As my feet hit the floor, I rushed to the cabin door to see what was going on outside. Upon opening the door, I was suddenly hit by more water than I have ever known in my life. It knocked me back on the floor of my cabin, and at that moment I tasted something I would taste often on the voyage—sea salt. I remember thinking: *I'm tasting the Pacific Ocean!* My mate managed to close the cabin door before the next huge wave hit.

Both of us rode out the storm in the cabin, not sleeping but throwing up and praying, each in our own way, that we would survive the night. It was too wild for me to remember that I was here courtesy of a thread that has guided me every mile of my life. I just held on and asked to be kept upright and afloat!

When light came the next day, the storm had quieted, and the sea, although anything but smooth, wasn't rocking quite as turbulently as it had been during the night. Because of the rough seas, there was no breakfast that morning, but as the passengers began to get their sea legs, we all began to settle in, grateful that we had withstood what we hoped was the worst the Pacific could throw at us.

There were so many adventures I experienced on this voyage that I am tempted to put in this book, but mercifully, I will share only a couple of things that reveal threads continuing to unfold before me.

Our first stop on this voyage of a lifetime was in Honolulu. Once the ship had docked, I was met by the then-ministers of Unity Church of Truth Hawaii, Revs. Phil and Dorothy Pierson. They greeted me with what I learned was a traditional flower lei and invited me to join them for breakfast under the famous banyan tree at the historic Moana Hotel.

I had not met Phil Pierson before, but his wife Dorothy (and here's the thread) was the minister in Toronto, Canada, who in 1944 greeted me and my family at Unity Church of Truth. She was my very first Unity minister and will always be one I love, honor, and revere. Dorothy, whom I had originally known as Dorothy O'Connor, was now Dorothy Pierson. She had been the one who was always there for me and had inspired me all through my ministry. She was the one who had taught me the "Prayer of Faith" and so much more.

After breakfast, Phil and Dorothy took me on a tour of their church, located on the slopes of world-famous Diamond Head. I immediately recall feeling somehow connected to this place.

I knew with a certainty I had never felt before that I would be returning often.

As the threads continued to wend their way through my life and Donna's, we would indeed return to this beautiful church, eventually with me as its senior minister and Donna as director of music and counseling. We served there from 1983 to 1991.

But that's another story. Back in 1964, after wishing Phil and Dorothy a fond *aloha* and boarding *Lakemba*, we again set sail for the open sea.

I remember we celebrated Christmas and New Year's on board. For some reason, I was made social director of the ship, which meant I had to come up with ways to keep the passengers entertained while we were at sea. On Christmas Eve, I and several others put "stockings" with candy and popcorn on each cabin door.

As we sailed south, the temperatures began heating up, and it became more and more difficult to sleep inside our cabins. There was no air conditioning.

One night, I decided to see whether I could find a breath of air out on deck. I took my pillow and went up to the bow, where I found an open spot that was free of cargo—stuff that was destined for Samoa, Fiji, or maybe all the way to Australia.

As I looked out on the ocean, I realized it was a sea of glass. Not a ripple or a wave to be seen. And the only sound I could hear was the soft swish at the bow and the slow murmur of the engines as the ship plied its way toward The Land Down Under.

I had never experienced a magical night like this. I put my pillow down on the deck and lay down and raised my glance skyward. The stars were out in full force that night, shining brightly in the heavens.

My eye hit upon something unfamiliar to one who had lived all his life in the Northern Hemisphere. It was a group of stars, a constellation that looked like a cross. I watched it with amazement until my eyes grew heavy and I drifted into sleep.

The next day, I asked the captain about the cross. He said in his immaculate British accent, "Oh, that's the Southern Cross. It's our navigation point of reference down here below the equator. It's the same thing that you chaps have in the Northern Hemisphere with your North Star."

At that moment, three things became a lot clearer:

1. Where I'd come from.
2. Where I was.
3. And where I was going.

The SS *Lakemba* docked in Sydney Harbor in early February 1964. I was met warmly by members of the Unity group. I named the Sydney ministry Unity Under the Southern Cross. I served as their minister for four years and during that time developed ministries in Brisbane and Melbourne, Australia, as well as two in New Zealand in Christchurch and Wellington.

While living and ministering in Australia, I began a correspondence with a woman in Michigan who was a Youth of Unity teacher. She was trying to get her YOU group off the ground and wanted to know whether I had any tips or suggestions, since I had both firsthand experience as a teen member of Youth of Unity and had worked with ministries that had successful groups for teens.

I sent her a list of ideas, and in one of her letters she mentioned she had a daughter living in Los Angeles and encouraged me to connect with her next time I was in L.A. Well, as a matter of fact, in 1966 I was planning a trip back to the mainland, as I had been invited by several Unity ministries to speak and share my adventures from Down Under. My first stop was to be Los Angeles.

The daughter met me at the airport, and we hit it off. We went to Disneyland and spent some quality time together. When it was time for me to move on to the other stops on my itinerary, we said our goodbyes, hugged, and vowed to stay in touch.

Among the ministries where I had been invited to speak was Detroit, Michigan. There I was greeted by the same woman I had hugged goodbye in Los Angeles a few days earlier. It just so happened that Detroit was her parents' home, and it just so happened she was visiting her parents. I was invited for dinner and there met her mother, the woman who had first written me about her Youth of Unity group.

I had a chance to spend more time with my new Los Angeles friend, then while I was touring, we kept in touch and things progressed for us. In short order, I found myself proposing to her. She accepted and we made plans to be married at Unity Village in Missouri, where we would spend some time in intense training to open a Silent Unity Prayer Ministry in Australia.

We were married in the Fillmore Chapel at Unity Village in late 1965 and moved into a cottage behind, would you believe, James Dillet Freeman's house. When we completed our Silent Unity training, we returned to the beautiful land Down Under.

Threads for Discussion ----------------------------------

1. What do you consider the greatest adventure of your life, that took you out of your comfort zone and into uncharted territory?

2. How did you adjust to this new environment or experience?

3. Are you still open for adventure? If so, what kind would you like to experience?

4. Do you have a "guiding star" that you reference to find your way in life?

HOW DO YOU GET TO CARNEGIE HALL?
Chapter 23

*The Relentless Stream of Truth has known no
boundaries. It has flowed through the minds
and hearts of both people of the church and
unchurched alike. We can find evidence of this
Relentless Stream of Truth in the thinking of
Plato and Socrates and Aristotle and others of the
Greek philosophers. We find it in St. Augustine,
St. Francis, Thomas Aquinas, Meister Eckhart,
and others among religious leaders. We find it
in Galileo, Copernicus, Newton, Einstein, and
others in the field of science. We find it in Hegel,
Kant, Schopenhauer, and others of "modern
philosophers." And we find it singing through
the words of poets, essayists like Shakespeare,
Browning, Tennyson, Carlyle, and Emerson. And
on it goes ...* —Eric Butterworth

It's taken me most of my adult life to finally get it through my
thick skull that the One I am currently referring to as the unifying
thread—the One I had been raised to affirm as One Presence and
One Power, God the Good, Omnipotent—has always been with
me and has always been there to heal, to guide, to prosper and
support me, no matter what. In the next chapters, I will share how
this thread of the Divine has shown up for me and for Donna in
even more ways time and time again. We are both conscious of the
spiritual connections that have shaped our lives. It is our hope
that you, too, can search and find the threads of heart and mind,
of love, life, and possibility that have been there within you—
many of them beneath the surface but nevertheless letting you
know that you've always been one with the One. All humanity has
always been one with the One.

Perhaps you've heard the story of a great musician being
stopped in New York City by a passerby who asked, "How do you

get to Carnegie Hall?" And the musician gave that famous reply, "Practice, practice, practice!"

Well, my journey to Carnegie Hall started when I was a 7-year-old kid living with my family in Toronto.

To tell this tale, I must reweave a thread introduced earlier.

In 1931 an Irishman by the name of Emmet Fox became the pastor of the Church of the Healing Christ in New York City, eventually called First Church of Divine Science. Because of the increasing size of his congregation, Fox had to find larger and larger venues in New York City. Having started in the ballroom of the Waldorf Astoria Hotel, Fox went on to meet in the world-famous Hippodrome, then finally Carnegie Hall. He most definitely got there through "practice, practice, practice." Fox went on to become one of the greatest mystics and religious teachers of the time, bringing new inspiration to America. He later died on a visit to Paris in 1951.

Okay, move forward to 1965. I had been in ministry several years and was returning from Australia to visit my parents in Toronto. While there, I received a phone call from a good friend and fellow Unity minister who was none other than Eric Butterworth. Butterworth, a fellow Canadian, had risen to become one of the foremost Unity ministers. He would soon become a prolific author of important spiritual books including *Discover the Power Within You*. Over the years, I had had the honor of working closely with him on various Unity committees and projects for what was called at the time the Association of Unity Churches. I had always admired his great mind, inspiring message, and warm personality.

Butterworth wanted to know whether I would be interested in guest speaking for him at his Unity ministry in New York City. He thought that since I had been living and ministering in Australia and New Zealand, I might have some interesting things to say to his congregation. He said he and his wife were going on vacation for a couple of weeks, and I could stay in their Bronx apartment while I was in the Big Apple.

Oh, and did I mention that his church services at the time were being held in a place called Carnegie Hall?

I've already shared the story of how my Aunt Hazel found her way to Carnegie Hall back when Emmet Fox was preaching there. She's the one who started taking shorthand notes of Fox's Sunday talks and mailing them to hundreds of people, including my mom. That was how my family found Unity. For me to be invited to speak in that hallowed hall as a 28-year-old minister was almost beyond belief. It truly was another strand of that amazing thread running in and through my life.

"Would I?" was my reply as I tried to keep my heart tucked into my chest. Not yet married, I asked Butterworth whether it would be all right if I brought my parents with me. "Sure thing," was his immediate reply.

In a few days, we packed up the family car and headed east from Toronto to New York City. It took two days to reach our destination, arriving on the Friday before my "debut" at Carnegie Hall.

We found Eric's apartment and settled in, then took in some of the sights and highlights of the Big Apple. As it happened, the World's Fair was going on in a place called Flushing Meadows. We also took a boat ride up the East River and down the Hudson. We climbed up the Empire State Building, and we dined at a place we had read about called Sardi's.

But we saved the best for Sunday morning. Without having to ask for directions, we arrived at the historic theater known worldwide as Carnegie Hall. Our eyes were all ga-ga as we entered the massive and lavish auditorium. After strategically seating my parents, I was ushered backstage to what was called the green room.

As I entered, I could barely catch my breath. On the walls of that room were portraits, autographs, and reviews of some of the biggest stars in the entertainment industry, as well as scientists, scholars, and politicians.

I was told to wait there until I was called to the stage. I could hardly believe this was happening to me, but it was.

I hurriedly looked over the notes I had prepared for my message, then a knock came at the door and a voice called out, "It's time, Reverend McClure. You're on!"

Walking from the green room to the stage seemed like the longest walk I had ever taken. Finally, I was in the wings of one of the most famous stages in the world. I walked out and looked at an almost-full auditorium. My knees began to buckle.

I immediately looked for my parents and there they were, giving me proud and reassuring looks that I found calming and centering. And then, as I looked at my mom, I thought of her sister, my dear Aunt Hazel, who discovered Emmett Fox and guided us to Unity. I silently blessed her for spinning out the thread that made this all possible.

Threads for Discussion

1. We all have threads from our childhood. Some are not happy or loving. Others set us on a course that is life-changing and transforming. What do you consider to be your most important childhood threads?

2. Are there people you have connected with over the years who have changed your life and set you on a course that altered your life?

3. List the most memorable moments of your life and why they are important to you.

SPOKANE CALLS

Chapter 24

'Tis sweet to feel by what fine-spun threads our
affections are drawn together. —Laurence Sterne

I returned to the U.S. from Australia, after which I was privileged to spend a few years ministering in Des Moines, Iowa. In 1970, I was called to become the minister of one of the Unity churches in San Francisco, California, on Ocean Avenue. It's still active today. And to this day, I love the Bay Area. I fell in love with its civility and open-mindedness, to say nothing of its beauty.

While I was there, I started a Unity group in Santa Rosa, north of San Francisco. On my trips up to Santa Rosa, I would pass a small airport in a town called Novato. On one of my journeys, I noticed a sign outside the airport that read: LEARN TO FLY!

I swung in there one afternoon and inquired about what it would take to become a licensed pilot. I was given the info and an invitation to take a free demonstration ride in a vintage biplane called a Stearman. I thought this a daunting choice for my first flight in a private plane, but, taking my seat behind the pilot and donning my leather helmet with goggles, my thoughts turned back to my dad, who was a flight instructor in Canada during the First World War. He used to tool around in a thing called a Sopwith Camel. I think that was Snoopy's air travel of choice later in *Peanuts*.

The pilot that day was to become my flight instructor. As we were warming up (more like *roaring* up in the Stearman), he turned back and said with a smirk on his face, "Are you ready to go up and defy death?"

His question startled me. But the demonstration flight was breathtaking and fabulous, and I didn't die. So I signed up for lessons. Every time Billy took me up, he would ask the same question about defying death. Little did he or I know there was a death-defying thread with my name on it decades ahead. I eventually got my pilot's license at Novato, California. Took a few solo flights around the state. Even took James Dillet Freeman up for a spin when he visited us in San Francisco. Now here was a connecting thread from my past! I was so thrilled to take him up, but as we were flying over the Golden Gate Bridge, I looked over and saw he had fallen asleep. So much for impressing my former mentor. Jim Freeman would continue to touch my life in the years before and after San Francisco, making speaking visits to some of my ministries.

One morning while ministering in San Francisco (I was there from 1970 to 1975), I was at home taking a shower, getting ready for a Sunday service, when the phone rang. I managed to hop out, wrap a towel around me, and get to the telephone in time to say hello to a woman who introduced herself as Sheri Barnard, president of the board of Unity Church of Truth in Spokane, Washington.

Bells and whistles went off when I realized this Sheri was the same woman I had first met as a teenager at a Youth of Unity Conference at Unity Village—Sheri Stovin. I had developed something of a crush on her but had lost track of her after our teenage years. Now here I was talking to her on the phone that morning in San Francisco. More threads were coming to the surface. She told me she was calling because she had heard some pretty good things about me and wondered if I might be interested in trying out for a ministerial opening that was about to occur in the Spokane church.

Having spent two years in Vancouver and having spoken in Spokane, I was eager to learn more. This was the same spot where Dr. Albert Grier had introduced his Church of Truth to America. Sheri informed me they had moved to a brand-new building some blocks from Grier's original church, and they now had a congregation of about 700.

Wow! I knew if I were to apply for that position, it would be a considerable step up for me, as I was currently serving about 200 in San Francisco. I thanked her and said I would pray about it. And, of course, you know the prayer I prayed: "Here am I, Lord. Use me!"

I was guided to call the executive director of the Association of Unity Churches. I wanted to get his take on making such an ambitious move geographically, as well as taking on greater responsibility than I'd ever had before.

He was forthright and honest with me. He felt this might be too big a step for me to take at that time. He was not in favor of my accepting the invitation. I thanked him, hung up the phone, and, once again, prayed my prayer. My answer came soon and sure.

In late 1974, I boarded a plane headed for Spokane to interview for the position. My wife stayed back in San Francisco, looking after our home, our dog, and working at her office job.

Sheri, the board president, was among those who greeted me at the airport, and I was transported to the outgoing minister's home in Spokane's South Hill district. After a tour of their lovely layout, my hosts took me outside to admire their gardens.

While we were standing on the front lawn, a sleek, silver sports car came tooling down the street in front of the house where the minister and I were standing. As the car zoomed past, I heard the car's horn beep and caught a glimpse of a gorgeous blonde in the driver's seat, driving her snazzy Nissan 240Z. She had the window open and waved to us as she drove by.

"Who was that?" I exclaimed to my host.

"Oh, that's Donna Anderson. She goes to our church. She lives just down the street. She teaches music in public schools, and on the side, plays viola in the Spokane Symphony. I suspect you'll run into her at church."

I made a private note to run into her at church.

And "run into her" I surely did. At a reception held for me by Donna's parents, I got a chance to meet this radiant, charming soul.

The next day at the Sunday service, she came through the receiving line after I had given my "tryout" sermon. She smiled, shook my hand, and said, "Great talk! I hope you get the job!" And then she was gone.

At that moment a beautiful, golden, unifying thread was beginning to unwind and wrap itself around me. A thread that would last a lifetime and, for all I know, beyond even that.

I landed the job in Spokane and my wife moved there with me

from San Francisco. We found a house near the church and moved in. Everything went smoothly for a couple of years until late 1977.

One evening, I came home from a busy day at the church to find my wife was absent. I didn't think much of it, but when she didn't arrive later in the evening, and then ultimately not even into the night, I felt a deep dread that something bad had happened to her. I tried calling some of her girlfriends, but no one had any information on her whereabouts. I called 911 to see if maybe she had been in an accident. They had no record of her being in an accident. I called both major hospitals to see if she had been admitted for a sudden illness. She was not in either hospital. Where was she?

I got no sleep that night. But I prayed that a thread would be revealed.

About 10 a.m. the following morning, she called. She said she had found a new person to love and she would not be coming back home ever again. As I listened to her, I felt my whole world come tumbling down around me. How could this be?

There had been no signs, no signals, no warnings that something like this was about to happen. I thought we had a solid, trusting relationship and here, all of a sudden, we had no relationship whatsoever.

After hanging up, I sulked around the house, still not believing this was happening. Later that day, I turned on the radio only to hear a song called "A House Is Not a Home," a 1964 ballad written by Burt Bacharach and Hal David. I couldn't believe I was actually living that music.

I remember taking a long walk through one of Spokane's great parks, Manito Park, and screaming at the top of my voice, "Here am I, Lord! What do I do now?"

The answer came in an amazing and unexpected way. A way that would change my life forever.

Before all this happened, my wife and I had organized, with the help of a travel agent, a two-week trip for 35 members of our Spokane congregation to Australia and New Zealand. We were planning to escort this group back to the place where we had lived and ministered for several years in the '60s. We were eager to see the progress these ministries had made in the decade after our time Down Under.

The group of travelers had already made their bookings, paid all their fees, and were packed, locked, loaded, and ready to head out on this journey. I knew I couldn't cancel the trip at this point. The only alternative was to find someone else to take on the responsibility of leading these folks on the trip.

After a great deal of prayer and searching, I finally found a couple who gladly agreed to escort the tour—Donna's parents, Dean and Almeda Campbell.

Okay, here we go—another thread unwinds.

The evening came for the tour's departure. I felt that, even though I was no longer escorting the group, the least I could do was to go to the airport and see them off.

At the gate, I gave the passengers a blessing and wished them a safe and happy trip. As I was waving farewell, I noticed there was one other person waving goodbye just 25 feet from where I was standing.

It was Donna.

Of course, she was there to see her parents off.

As the last passenger disappeared down the departure ramp, I turned and looked at Donna. She was looking back at me and smiling. Immediately, I felt what I knew to be the thread drawing us closer and closer.

And then she said the words that would forever join us together for the rest of this life's journey and beyond. "Do you want to go have a drink?" After I agreed, she said: "I don't usually extend invitations like I just did!"

We talked, we laughed, we giggled, and we had a drink. Or maybe it was two.

I had a class to teach that night at the church. I made it and taught the class, but don't ask me what I said.

In the days that followed, my first wife and I settled our affairs, divided the furniture, the pots and pans, and all the stuff we had accumulated in 12 years together, hugged, and went our separate ways. We were divorced in 1977.

During that time, I did not feel led to date or seek female company. I had been burned by my last relationship and still needed time to heal. But as the days passed, I began to feel I was once again free to open the door to female companionship. I had gone through my mourning period and started to open my heart and mind once again.

My thoughts kept coming back to my brief encounter with Donna. As part of the agreement that Donna's parents would escort the group to Australia and New Zealand, I had agreed to live in their home and look after their cat and their plants. To my delight, every few days, Donna would come by to see how I was doing and make sure I was taking good care of the house, the cat, and the plants. Still, nothing developed between us until something started to develop between us.

There finally came a day, some months after my divorce, when I mustered up my courage and asked her for a date. To my joy she accepted. And from then on, our relationship deepened and grew. Our conversations also deepened and grew.

After we had been dating for a month, I called her one day and told her I'd found this cozy, romantic little restaurant I wanted us to check out. It was about a two-hour drive from Spokane. Would she be game to try it? Without hesitation, she said, "Sure!"

On a Friday night in late October, we drove north from Spokane to a small town in Idaho called (are you ready for this?) Hope.

The restaurant I was looking for was the Lighthouse, situated on the shores of beautiful Lake Pend Oreille. (Later, I discovered this spot was where the famous Litehouse salad dressings originated.)

I had made reservations ahead of time and requested a table by the window so we could look out at the lake. But when we arrived, the host told us the restaurant was extremely crowded and the only table left was in the middle of the restaurant—right square in a sea of people.

He apologized, and reluctantly we took our seats and ordered some wine.

136

It was obvious this was not the romantic start I had anticipated, but nevertheless, the tapestry was weaving its way in and through our lives.

Then, one of the great moments in the history of David and Donna happened. I looked over at the radiant creature across the table, and without planning, without thinking, without rehearsing, and even without praying my favorite prayer, I spouted out: "Donna, will you marry me?"

I had not planned to pop the question that night. I had seen Donna a few times in church, playing her viola at the Spokane Symphony, and walking across the street between an elementary school where she taught music and the corner store to get a Twinkie. We'd dated for a very short period—certainly not enough to establish a solid relationship that might withstand anything like a full commitment.

But here I was, blurting out the age-old question.

There was a startled look on her face momentarily. But the startle turned to smile, and she said, "David, I'm not exactly sure I heard what you just said because it's so loud in here, but the answer is yes!"

And so, on that night, in a town called Hope, without warning, without an engagement ring, without a lot of time together, our lives became intertwined.

Donna and I were married at Unity Church of Truth in June 1978.

At first glance, it didn't seem as if Donna and I had any kind of a thread going for us. A wave from a sports car, a wave to our departing travelers at the airport, and a yes! at the dinner table in a place called Hope. Not a whole lot to start a lifelong relationship, would you agree?

But in the following days, the origins of our commonality and the spiritual threads that had woven in, through, and around us began to reveal themselves. This is such an astonishing story, I can hardly believe it's true. But it is and here goes.

I have already related the section of the thread that includes the late, great Dr. Albert Grier. A woman named Irma Wells carried on his Church of Truth ministry in Spokane, later naming it Unity Church of Truth. The church occupied a building at the corner of Sixth and Jefferson on the South Hill. This had been the spiritual home for Church of Truth and Unity folks in Spokane for many, many years. And among those who attended there was a 10-year-old Donna, her brother Paul, and her parents. They started going there because Donna's father had cancer and needed some of the Unity healing message.

Then in 1963 Rev. Daniel Perin became their minister. It just so happens this was the same year I was ministering a few hundred miles north in Vancouver, B.C. Dan and I had developed a good friendship from our days in ministerial training at Unity School. We had both worked in Silent Unity during our instructional years and had served together on various committees and task forces over the years.

One day Dan called and told me he was going to be out of town for a couple of days, asking if I would be interested in speaking at Unity Church of Truth in Spokane. I said that I would and eventually flew down to Spokane from Vancouver.

As it happened, this turned out to be a whole other strand of the Spokane thread that was coming into my awareness and into my life.

This would be my one and only time in this hallowed building that carried so much history and so many threads of connection with so many students of Truth and Unity. It was the cornerstone of the lives and spiritual development of so, so many, including Donna and her parents, to say nothing of the teenager I met back in Youth of Unity, Sheri Stovin Barnard.

And now I introduce the next piece in that thread. Dan Perin eventually left Unity Church of Truth and was succeeded by Revs. Phil and Mary Stovin, Sheri's parents.

Are you seeing how the thread unwinds?

Just to spell it out again, not only for you but for me, because I can hardly believe it: Phil and Mary had a daughter named Sheri Stovin. This daughter turned out to be the same beautiful blonde from my Youth of Unity Conference at Unity Village. And this is the same woman who became the president of the board of Unity Church of Truth and called to invite me up from San Francisco to try out for the Spokane ministry.

Are you still following me? If you're having a hard time following this, I know what you're going through. I have been dealing with this all my life.

Sheri was to meet and marry (in 1969) a well-known architect in Spokane named Kim Barnard, who went on to design and build the brand-new Unity Church of Truth facility where it stands today on the corner of 29th and Bernard in the South Hill neighborhood of Spokane. The new church building was completed in 1974. I arrived to be the minister in 1975.

Oh, one other note of interest: Sheri went on to become mayor of Spokane.

So, when I arrived in 1975, not only did I inherit a beautiful, new church building but an amazing and enthusiastic congregation of 700. And to top it all off, I met, courted, and married dear Donna in 1978.

But wait! There's more! I'm just getting warmed up.

Early in our married life, I learned that Donna was actually a fourth-generation member of the Unity family. Her great-grandfather attended the original Church of Truth. His daughter, Donna's grandmother, helped the church set up Unity classes in Lewiston, Idaho, for Irma Wells.

Donna's grandmother, of course, gave birth to Donna's mother, who became president of the board of the newly built Unity Church of Truth at 29th and Bernard in 1980. And that woman gave birth to—you guessed it—my dear, dear Donna!

Can you believe all these connections? Can you see the threads? They follow decades of commitments, individual and collective choices, and dedicated service to Unity. And what is even more amazing is that all of this follows the same threads that Charles and Myrtle Fillmore created more than a century ago when they were led to introduce this spiritual movement called Unity.

Can you see that it was no accident I met and married Donna and grabbed onto the thread that was to unite the two of us together along with many of the early elements of the entire Truth movement? I must believe that all of this was the work of—you guessed it—the guiding thread.

This morning as I was writing, another thread that has proven to be especially important to Donna and me came to mind.

First, I wish to add a quotation from a teaching that Donna and I believe is a companion to our longtime thread of connection to the Fillmores and Unity. I am talking about *A Course in Miracles*.

Here's one of our favorite quotes from this amazing book:

"Trials are but lessons that you failed to learn presented once again, so where you made a faulty choice before you now can make a better one, and thus escape all pain that what you chose before has brought to you. In every difficulty, all distress, and each perplexity Christ calls to you and gently says, 'My brother, choose again'" (*A Course in Miracles*, Text-31, VIII. 3:1-2).

This verse and so many more from what is described as a "complete self-study spiritual thought system" have become an integral thread on our spiritual journey. And how this thread became a part of our connection happened like this:

It was 1976, not long after I had begun my ministry at Spokane Unity. One day, I arrived at the church office early and, opening my office door, I glanced down at my desk and was surprised to find this rather large blue book sitting there. I read the title. It said *A Course in Miracles*. Looking inside, I discovered it was hot off the press, having been published in 1976. I remember thumbing through a few pages and reading some of the text. My first impression was, *Hmm, this is pretty weird.* I took the book and delivered it to the church secretary, suggesting she deposit it in our church library.

About a month later, the same scenario unfolded. I arrived in my office to find another copy of *A Course in Miracles* smiling at me from my desk. I thought it strange that it would appear again. My first inclination was to dispose of it in the same manner as the first copy. But then a voice inside of me said: "Open once again and read!" So I did. I read the very words that I quoted to you above. I recall feeling as though something physically, emotionally, mentally, and spiritually shifted inside of me and, in that moment, I was made different—made new by what I had just read.

I decided to check out the book with a minister friend of mine. Rev. J. Sig Paulson, I learned, had written an article about the book titled "Unity. You. And *A Course in Miracles.*" I called him, and he said it was an amazing book that I should check out. So I did.

Move ahead a few months. Donna and I were invited to attend and participate in a retreat on the western side of Washington state at a place called Menucha Retreat and Conference Center. The word *menucha* means "rest and peaceful tranquility" in Hebrew.

The retreat was sponsored by Young Adults of Unity, a group of women and men in their late teens and early 20s who attended Unity ministries in the region. The featured guests, who were to lead us in workshops and music, were unknown to us at the time, but the thread with these two men and one woman would stay tied to us for many years to come, both in Spokane and in Hawaii. Their names were Oman, Shanti, and Charley.

Their music was all original material they had created from words used in *A Course in Miracles*. Donna and I were spellbound by the music and by the message we heard. Once again, in that moment, we both felt our lives elevated to a new level on the spiritual ladder. We would hear from these dear people, both in person and on recordings, for years to come.

Interestingly, and here's another of the unifying threads, one of the participants in this retreat was a young woman by the name of Clare Austen from the Portland, Oregon, Young Adults of Unity. We got to know her quite well during the retreat, and as we said farewell to her at the closing ceremonies, we had no knowledge of how she would tie into the Unity thread that was continuing to develop ahead of us.

It was more than 30 years later, in 2009, when Donna and I returned to Spokane after serving six years in the Unity Windward ministry in Hawaii. As we stepped back into our home church that day on Spokane's South Hill, we were greeted by the woman who had become the senior minister—Clare Austen, whom we had met some three decades earlier at the *A Course in Miracles* retreat! Now is that a thread or what?

Threads for Discussion

1. How far back can you trace your religious threads? How far back can you trace your spiritual threads? Is there a difference between your early religious threads and your current spiritual threads? What makes them the same? What makes them different?

2. How far back do your memories of your connections with family, significant relationships, or associations go?

3. Do you feel that you are currently in touch with either the healing thread of your heart or the guiding thread of your mind and that your life is developing with a clear sense of purpose and direction?

PASSING ON OR PASSING OVER

Chapter 25

Whatever may happen to you was prepared for you
from all eternity; and the implication of causes was
from eternity spinning the thread of your being.
—Marcus Aurelius

It was late November of 1977. I was invited to guest speak at the Unity ministry in Missoula, Montana. I had never been to the great state of Montana, so I readily agreed to drive the 198 miles over to Missoula very early on a Sunday morning to speak at their 11 a.m. service.

I knew there was a mountain pass between Idaho and Montana called Lookout Pass. I checked the weather report before leaving, and it indicated the pass was clear with no snow on Interstate 90.

I left before morning light and headed east. I brought extra coffee to keep me bright-eyed and bushy-tailed throughout the morning. I thought I would arrive in plenty of time for the service. Listening to some great rock music on the radio, I went over the thoughts I hoped to impart to the folks in the Treasure State.

I passed through Idaho and headed up the western slope to the top of Lookout Pass. This early in the morning, the road was dark in my headlights, but as far as I could ascertain, it was clear. I was hurrying along at a pretty good clip, a tad above the listed speed limit I must admit.

Little did I know that my assumption about the condition of the highway would prove to be very, very wrong.

After reaching the summit of the pass (elev. 4,711 feet) and heading down the eastern slope, almost immediately I began to feel movement beneath me as the car began to swing and sway. I lightly applied the brakes but that only made matters worse. Then without any warning, my car began to spin totally out of my control. I was hurtling down the mountain pass, helpless to influence the trajectory of my little Toyota Celica.

I remember hearing of people having "come to Jesus" moments when they saw their whole life flash in front of them. But now, I was only experiencing this moment in time. There was absolutely nothing I could do except to pray: "Here am I, Lord, save me!" Sliding off the side of the road and over a cliff to the rocky canyon below seemed inevitable. The end of everything was all that lay ahead for me.

After my last, desperate prayer, I closed my eyes and waited.

But then, all I heard was loud scraping and scratching. And then nothing. My car had miraculously stopped all motion. Instead of experiencing what I had been dreading, I opened my eyes to see that my car had hit a snowbank on the westbound side of the highway. It had crunched and grinded, making the worst noises I have ever heard. But it finally came to a screeching, scraping halt next to the guardrail on the opposite side of the highway.

After that, there was nothing but silence.

Checking my body, I ascertained that I still had all my essential physical parts in place. I attempted to open the driver's side door, but at first it resisted. *Oh boy,* I thought. *I'm stuck here for the rest of my life!* But as I pushed a little harder, the door gave way and slowly opened on a large snowbank. I was able to crawl out and stand on my own two feet to observe the damage, which I expected to be extensive. I glanced over the railing to the valley hundreds of feet below. Without the guardrail and the snowbank, I would have been toast.

I noticed the driver's door had a long scrape in it but wasn't bent out of shape. Carefully walking around to the passenger side of the car, to my happy surprise I found no obvious damage. All the wheels were intact, and, as much as I looked, I could find nothing out of place.

Nothing, that is, until I went to the rear of the car and noticed something very important was missing. It was my Washington state license plate. It had vanished and was nowhere in sight.

Well, I thought, *I am so, so grateful to be alive in one piece with most of my car intact. That's a small price to pay for once again defying death with still enough time to make the Sunday service in Missoula.*

But what about the missing license plate? I did love that license plate. It was not your run-of-the-mill license plate with numbers and letters that meant nothing. I had a special plate with one word especially important to me. A word that was my destiny, my ministry, and my vanity. The license plate simply said: UNITY. Could I drive without any rear license plate?

I figured I'd try to hunt it down, since the Montana Highway Patrol might stop me with a few questions. I wandered over to the huge pile of snow by the guardrail. I hadn't brought any snow boots, so here I was in my "Sunday go-to-meetin'" shoes and outfit, trudging through the snowbanks. I found nothing.

Just then a car came up the highway from the Montana side and stopped nearby. A young couple got out and asked what I was doing and whether they could help me. I told them about my spinout and that the only thing missing from the car was my license plate.

This young man and woman began their own stomp through the snow. It was not more than five minutes later when one of them yelled, "Hey! Is this your license plate?" I looked at the piece of metal they were holding up and said, "Oh, my God! That's it!"

They came back to the car and handed it to me. Then, the young man said, "Unity, eh?"

I said, yes. I told them I was the Unity minister at Unity Church of Truth in Spokane.

They looked at one another with wide eyes, then broke into laughter. They asked, "Unity Church of Truth? You aren't, by any chance, Rev. David McClure, are you?"

I said that I was.

They looked at me with delight and proceeded to tell me that they were on their way from Missoula, Montana, to get married in Spokane at Unity Church of Truth by a guy named Rev. David McClure. The wedding was supposed to happen tomorrow!

I kid you not, this is a true story.

I went over and hugged them and thanked them for finding my license plate and assured them I'd be back in Spokane for our 2 p.m. appointment tomorrow to tie their knot and complete this amazing, phenomenal, miraculous thread of not only defying death but finding love and Unity on the side of a mountain.

I drove on to Missoula and had another little story to tell for my morning sermon.

Threads for Discussion ——————————————————————

1. What is the closest you have come to your own demise? How did you survive?

2. Do you have any synchronicities or "coincidences" that you remember vividly?

3. Do you tell the story of these events, and are others still astounded to hear about them?

THE OPERA HOUSE CAPER
Chapter 26

Everything is connected to everything else.
—Barry Commoner

Back around the same year that the new Unity Church of Truth opened on the South Hill in Spokane, another building down by the Spokane River opened with great fanfare and hoopla. It was called the Spokane Opera House. Today it's known as the First Interstate Center for the Arts. It is a big, beautiful structure that seats about 2,600 people.

One of the first people to perform in this enormous hall was my wife Donna, playing viola in the Spokane Symphony.

During the time before our marriage and continuing long afterward, I frequented this magnificent building quite often. I would sit up in the balcony and look down at the orchestra, and my eyes would focus on one young woman whose hair shone and glistened in the theater lights. How blessed I was to now have her standing beside me on Sunday mornings at Unity. The light shines from her very presence. She was and is a jewel.

A group of folks began planning our annual Easter service, which is always a special occasion for Unitics. We honor the resurrection of Jesus, threading it into the overcoming that everyone will experience in their lives.

A cornerstone of the Unity teachings that weaves and unifies us all the way back to Charles and Myrtle Fillmore is that Unity is the practical application of the teachings of Jesus. That's our message, and we want to get it out to as many people as we can. Charles Fillmore used to call Unity "practical Christianity" because to benefit from Jesus' teachings you must practice them. How do you gain spiritual consciousness? Practice. Practice. Practice.

So as our Easter planning group was talking, someone in the group brought up a wild and crazy idea. He explained that there were many people in Spokane who needed a practical application of the Easter message but had no affiliation with a church or a

147

religion. These folks, he said, were all over the city. Wouldn't it be great if we could reach out to more of them? What would we think of having Easter services at a venue that is centrally located and seats a ton of people? "Where would that be?" we all asked. "Well," he said, "it's the Opera House."

Whoa! The Opera House? A few in the group said, "You've got to be crazy!" Others said, "That's impossible. They're not going to let a relatively small and little-known church the likes of ours take over the city's prize auditorium!"

We decided we'd pray about it. And so, of course, the affirmation I had everyone use was: *Here am I, Lord. Use me!*

After we had prayed and meditated on this for about 10 minutes, I said, "Amen."

Then someone said, "Well, we'd better get busy. If we're going to have Easter at the Opera House, there's a whole lot of planning ahead of us. We'd better get our act together!"

And that was that. There being no more naysayers or doubting Thomases in the group, we rolled up our sleeves and began to prepare for this tremendous undertaking. Everyone left the meeting believing we could pull this off. They didn't know how, but they knew when, where, and why.

And so, the church went into gear.

The first thing, of course, was to contact the folks at the Opera House to see if they would even entertain the thought of having us there on Easter Sunday. To our surprise and joy, they said, "Yes! The Opera House is not being used on Easter Sunday and we would love to have you use our facility."

There were reams of paperwork and deposits necessary to seal the deal, but all of that seemed to flow more smoothly than anyone expected. Pretty soon, we had a contract in our hot little hands and were off to the races.

We had teams for ushering, for music, for staging, for advertising, and for everything else we could imagine that might be needed to put this extravaganza together. We began to feel excited that we just might be able to pull off a Sunday morning service that would blow the socks off the people of Spokane. We would even have folks dressed like Easter bunnies and baby chicks to greet folks as they entered the building. We had meetings on top of meetings. It was exhausting but thrilling. The folks of Unity Church of Truth had come together as never before.

And so, on Easter Sunday in 1977, our planning team and participants gathered early for one last run-through and coordination. Finally, we opened the doors of the great and mighty Opera House. We put all our planning and all our hard work in the hands of the guiding thread and in the hands of the One whose day of new beginnings we were to honor that day.

And people started to come, first in small numbers, but then in larger numbers. At that time we had been broadcasting our Sunday services on radio and started plugging "Easter at the Opera House" a month before Easter. We also bought bigger and snazzier ads on the local newspaper's church page. We had great graphics and our ad stood out among the other church ads on the page. And so, to our utter amazement and joy, 10 minutes before the service was to begin, the great hall was filled!

It was the largest church service in the city that Sunday or any Sunday for five years. It was the greatest coming together that Unity Church of Truth had ever experienced. It was the most fun, the most inspirational, and the most work I had ever been involved with. The service went off without a hitch.

Immediately, we started planning for next Easter.

Months later, after our first Opera House service, I found myself back in my familiar balcony seat in the auditorium, looking down at my radiant Donna, with her shining golden locks, playing her viola in the Spokane Symphony Orchestra, and feeling more at home in that building than I ever had before.

We went on to hold a total of five Easter services there while I was minister, and the church carried on with a couple more after Donna and I left for Hawaii. New threads were made, strengthened, discovered, and new friends were brought together.

Threads for Discussion ——————————————————————————

1. Have you ever been involved in the planning and execution of an event that seemed larger than life? What event was that?

2. Did you have doubts about pulling it off? If so, how did you overcome those doubts?

3. Is there a project looming in your life today that seems daunting but that you would love to see completed? What is that project? How are you going to go about finishing it?

ALOHA! HAWAII CALLS

Chapter 27

*The only good thing about leaving Hawaii is that
you really appreciate it when you return.* —John
Richard Stephens, *The Hawaii Bathroom Book*

After watching a rerun of the movie, *South Pacific*, we talked about
loving the Hawaiian Islands. Donna had visited there with her
mother some years ago, and I, of course, had experienced Hawaii
when I steamed across the Pacific from Vancouver, Canada, to
Sydney, Australia. I had met the Unity ministers in Honolulu,
one of whom was my first Unity minister when I was 7 years old
in Toronto. Dorothy Pierson and her husband Phil had taken me
to visit their ministry at Unity Church of Hawaii on the slopes of
a dormant volcano called Diamond Head. Donna and I both had
tasted the sweet, exotic Hawaiian experience, and both of us had a
desire and, I might say, a calling to return to the islands sometime
in the future.

A week after we watched *South Pacific*, I got a call from a friend
who had been my roommate while we were both at ministerial
school years before. His name was Rev. Stan Hampson.

Coincidentally, he had served as the senior minister at Unity
Church of Hawaii from 1967 to 1975. He had since moved back
to the mainland, but he wanted me to know there might be an
opening at the Honolulu church.

So the call of the islands surfaced once again for us. It was
surely a thread we felt compelled and guided to follow. I called
and talked with the board president at Unity Church of Hawaii. He
said yes indeed there was an opening, and I could apply by going
through the Field Department at Unity World Headquarters.

I could hardly wait to get off the phone so I could call the Field
Department. They said they would send me the forms.

I shared what had transpired with Donna, and we both jumped
with glee and did a little Hawaiian dance around the living room. I
had been in Spokane now for eight wonderful years. Spokane held
many memories for us, with so many threads connecting us there

151

to so many events and people. But we both were feeling a nudge to make a change.

In a few days, the application papers arrived. I filled them out and mailed them to Hawaii. I waited for their response. I waited and I waited. I recalled that there was something in the islands called "Hawaiian Time," which translated means, "Whenever, brah!"

Finally, after eight weeks of waiting, I received a call from the board president in Honolulu, saying the board of directors had voted to give me a tryout for the senior minister position. He asked whether I could come on a certain day (they would pay for my airfare) and told me that my wife was invited as well.

Within a few days, we flew off to Hawaii. The good folks at the church warmly greeted us, covered us with flowered leis, and put us up in a local hotel by the beach. *Ahhhhhhh!*

Once we had checked in, we changed into our bathing suits and flip-flops and headed for Waikiki Beach. It was love at first dip! Swimming in that warm, Pacific water sealed the deal for us. We felt we truly belonged in Hawaii.

When we arrived at Unity Church of Hawaii, I felt the same spirit of *aloha* I had felt years earlier when being escorted there by the Piersons. It felt so right to be there.

The next few days were filled with interviews with board and staff. I spoke at three services Sunday morning and Donna led the meditations.

Expecting a decision near the end of our stay, we were disappointed to learn they had not made up their minds at this point. There were two other candidates, and they weren't sure which of us would be the right choice.

We thanked them for their hospitality and flew back to Spokane. We said nothing to our congregation about our real purpose for going to Hawaii, simply telling them we had a beautiful vacation and enjoyed our stay.

A week later, we still hadn't heard a word from Hawaii. And then another week passed. And another. I called the board president, and he said, "David, I'm sorry but the jury is still out."

To say that we were frustrated and disappointed was an understatement. I decided it was time to take matters into my own hands. I boarded a plane heading to Honolulu, rented a car, checked into a hotel, and took some time to walk the beach to think and pray. And by now, you know the prayer: "Here am I, Lord. Use me!"

The next day was Sunday, and I showed up at the service. There were a lot of wide eyes looking at me as I walked into the open-air sanctuary. No one had expected me. No one had invited or encouraged me.

The service was beautiful with lots of Hawaiian music and aloha spirit. Afterward the president of the board approached me and asked why I had shown up there in Hawaii. I told him I had not heard anything about their choice for the new minister, and I thought I would come and see for myself what might be holding up the process.

He relayed to me that the board simply could not make up its mind regarding a new minister. He said there were some who wanted me, and others wanted one of the other candidates.

He hurriedly called a few of the board members to huddle with him while I enjoyed the generous display of food and refreshments served after the 11 a.m. service, the last of the morning.

Thirty minutes later, the board president found me. He had a big smile on his face.

He said, "Up until today, we were deadlocked on our choice for a new senior minister. But since you took the time and spent the money to show up and demonstrate your interest in this position, the board has voted, and David, we want you to be our new minister!"

Aloha and thank you, guiding thread!

I thanked the board and blessed the people who would be our new Unity family.

A little history on this ministry is worthy of attention at this point. Back in 1930, a small group of earnest seekers of Truth found each other in Hawaii. They began to study together the teachings

153

of Charles and Myrtle Fillmore and to communicate with Unity World Headquarters.

This group had a vision of having their own Unity church with their own ordained Unity minister. Their prayers were answered in 1937—the year I was born—when Marie Parker Handley heard the call to service, left her position at Unity World Headquarters, and made her steamship pilgrimage to Honolulu to start this new ministry. From 1937 to 1963—the year before I arrived by freighter—this church's name was and still is Unity Church of Hawaii.

And so, yet another unifying thread from the Fillmores was added to my spiritual journey and the journey of so many Unity students throughout the world. Donna and I moved to Honolulu and served in that ministry from 1983 to 1991.

Threads for Discussion ———————————————————————

1. Have you ever had to take matters into your own hands to get some movement in a situation that was not resolved? What was that situation, and how did you bring it to a conclusion?

2. Did you ever branch out into a lifestyle or profession that was quite different from what you had been originally trained to do? What was that new thread, and how did you fare?

3. What did you learn from that experience?

DANCING GROUND OF THE SUN
Chapter 28

*The Hopi Indians thought that the world's
religions each contained one spiritual thread, and
that these threads are always seeking each other,
wanting to join. When all the threads are finally
woven together, they will form a rope that will pull
us out of this dark cycle of history and into the next
realm.*—Elizabeth Gilbert

As often as I have felt called to minister in a Unity church, there
also seems to be a need sometimes to leave ministerial duties
behind and see what else the guiding thread has in store.

There was a period, after I had been doing ministry for almost
20 years, when, for no reason, Donna and I looked at each other
and said, in effect, "I wonder what else there is in this world for us
to do or be? Is there anything besides ministry?"

The answer came swiftly when we said our final *alohas* to the
good people of Honolulu and headed back to the mainland in
Southern California during the summer of 1991.

We picked up our car, which a steamship line in Honolulu
had shipped over earlier to Long Beach, California. From there,
we decided, with no destination in mind, to just go with the flow
and head out and see what Spirit had in store for us. We had never
frequented the southwestern United States but had always had a
fascination with that part of the country.

We drove through Palm Springs, spent some time in Flagstaff,
and marveled at the Grand Canyon. I was able to show Donna
exactly where my car had died on my way north to Vancouver back
in 1962. Since then, I've had a few more spiritual experiences that
involved car trouble.

We especially loved Sedona, Arizona, and found ourselves
sorely tempted to pitch our tent there. We loved the legends, the
vortexes, and the beauty of this remarkable town, but for some
reason, it just was not for us.

We loved Durango and Grand Junction in Colorado but no, they were also not our spot.

Finally, we drove into Santa Fe, New Mexico, the Land of Enchantment, and we were hooked. I hesitate to describe Santa Fe because I cannot possibly do it justice. It is the most remarkable town we had ever seen.

Our inner guidance was to stop there and become residents of this one-of-a-kind location on the map of the United States.

We hunted for a place to live and discovered a horse ranch on the outskirts of town with miles of scenery, friendly neighbors, and room for us and our three pets. Oh, did I mention our pets? Part of the family that escorted us from Spokane to Honolulu consisted of our Sheltie dog, Angel, and our two Siamese cats, Tiger and Punky. Their first four months in Hawaii had been spent in a shelter where animals that came from off-islands had to be quarantined. It was a tough time for us and for them, even though we took great pains to visit them in their caged home as often as we could.

We had left them with a friend in Hawaii while we made this reconnoitering/sightseeing trip around the Southwest looking for our next place to land. Once we settled on the ranch in Santa Fe, we sent for the animals and soon greeted them in Albuquerque.

And so, here we were, ensconced in this little ranch house out among the piñon pines, sagebrush, and coyotes. What next?

Next was a plan and a direction that seemed to come out of nowhere. It seems that OPOPGGO wanted us to stretch our abilities and envision something far beyond anything we had done. I remember a quote from one of Robert Browning's poems that goes: "A man's reach should exceed his grasp, or what's a heaven for?"

Well, our reach was about to exceed our grasp. What if we did something that was entirely different from church ministry? Like what, you may ask? Well, how about a bed-and-breakfast?

A what? What did we know about running a business? What did we know about greeting overnight guests, serving them breakfast, making beds, cleaning toilets, and doing a whole bunch of laundry? Well, not much, to be honest. Maybe I could cook up a few light things for breakfast. And Donna was certainly good at running and organizing an office. But that is about all we had going for us.

So once again—this time in unison—came our prayer of prayers: "Here we are, God. Use us!"

We began by looking for a suitable piece of property for our outrageous venture. After a lengthy search, we finally discovered a group of *casitas* near the popular Plaza in downtown Santa Fe. This had location, charm, and a price that was within our budget.

And so, the McClure B&B was born! To this day, I can hardly believe we took this on.

After extensive remodeling and the addition of an office/apartment for Donna, me, and the three pets, and a lot of paperwork to comply with Santa Fe's strict laws for operating a B&B, plus their historical guidelines, we left our Santa Fe ranch home to become the proprietors of this cute little resting place for weary tourists who wanted to see the amazing sights of Santa Fe. For a final touch we brought in a local artist who painted Southwestern images on the adobe walls of the four casitas that would house our guests.

We named our little B&B Dancing Ground of the Sun. In reading up on Santa Fe, we learned that the original settlers here, the Pueblo Native Americans, had named this magical place because of the amazing dancing light that emanated from the sun shining on the land. And so, once again, my "dance with the sun" was about to play out in my travels with the big orange ball that followed me everywhere.

Finally, we were ready to open for business. Initially, the hospitality team consisted of Donna and me and the pets. Our B&B consisted of four casitas, aptly named *Kokopelli*, Buffalo Dancer, Corn Dancer, and Rainbow Dancer.

We were so excited when we had our first booking. It happened about a month after we opened. We gushed over our first couple. You would think that royalty had arrived at our door. We enthusiastically escorted them to our deluxe casita, Kokopelli. They stayed for three nights, and we were in heaven. Another thread we had not expected had been spun.

We patiently waited for more reservations; however, none were forthcoming. We knew it would take a while for word to get out. After all, we were the new kids in town. Finally, bookings started to trickle in, then pour in, which is where Donna and I discovered that running a B&B—running any business, for that matter—was going to be a 24/7 commitment.

We worked our tails off! Donna looked after the bookings, the registrations, and the check-in and check-out side of the business. I cooked and spent time spreading the word all over town about what a great place Dancing Ground of the Sun was—and still is, although today it's called by a different name with different owners. Our establishment was positioned perfectly within walking distance of the famous Plaza in Santa Fe, so it seemed as if it would be a tourist magnet.

Our breakfast consisted of homemade blueberry muffins, fruit, juice, coffee, and tea. The muffin recipe was one I had discovered years before in a small book that someone had given me. It was simple but oh so delicious, and the guests raved about the muffins. We would put the breakfast tray in the refrigerator in each room in the late afternoon so the occupants would have it ready to eat the next morning.

Most of the folks who stayed with us were congenial and happy to be nestled in our beautiful nest. However, there were a few who, no matter how you tried to please them, complained about this and that.

After six months, Dancing Ground was humming along but we obviously needed extra help. So we hired our first employee to take care of the unending stream of laundry that was always piling up.

One day, a reporter from the local newspaper came by and asked us for a tour of Dancing Ground. He asked many questions, took some notes, and thanked us for showing him around.

About a month later, we discovered this piece in the Santa Fe newspaper:

"At the edge of Santa Fe's downtown district, you can find a group of uniquely decorated 1930s-era pueblo and territorial style bungalows, some with kitchens and kiva fireplaces. The casitas and rooms at Dancing Ground of the Sun have been decorated with handcrafted Southwestern-style furniture made by local craftspeople. Each is classically decorated and named after a fanciful figure from the rich lore and past of the area. Dancing Ground of the Sun is located within walking distance of the historic Santa Fe Plaza and approximately 10 miles from Santa Fe Municipal Airport. The quaint property has been voted by *Santa Fe Magazine* as Most Local Charm."

Wow! What an endorsement! What encouragement! What a thread of possibility!

The bookings came thick and fast after that. Pretty soon, we were filled to capacity almost every night. We had to hire a second employee to keep up with the constant flow of tourists who stopped at our B&B for some R&R.

While we were busy, booked, and bountifully prospered by the business, we began to discover that it was taking its toll on the McClures. After two years, we realized that, although we had shown we could successfully run a bed-and-breakfast business, this was only a diversion from our true calling. Once again, we began to find ourselves praying the prayer that had always pointed us where we needed to be: "Here we are, Lord. Use us."

One very busy day at Dancing Ground, I received a call from Rev. Max Lafser, a Unity minister I had known for years. He was currently ministering in the Lehigh Valley of Pennsylvania in a small town called Emmaus. He relayed to me that he was retiring from ministry and the congregation of Unity Church of Lehigh Valley had asked him for a recommendation for who might replace him. He said he immediately thought of me. This call came out of the blue, but it seemed to be happening at the right time.

I thanked him and said I would pray about it.

Three months later, I visited the church in Emmaus, tried out, fell in love with the congregation, and was accepted as the new, incoming minister. We sold our dear Dancing Ground and moved to Pennsylvania. While we had proved to ourselves that we had it in us to successfully run a small B&B, we knew in our hearts that our main thread was ministry.

Threads for Discussion —————————————————————

1. Have you ever diverted from your chosen path or profession to try your hand at something else? Describe what the "diversion" was and the result of this endeavor.

2. What lessons did you learn from taking this alternative path and following this different thread?

3. Is there possibly a new and different field of expression that you would love to try? What would it take for you to move in that direction? Are you willing to take the steps necessary to give this a go?

THE ROAD TO EMMAUS
Chapter 29

The open road is there; it will always be there.
You just have to decide when to take it.
—Chris Humphrey

The town of Emmaus, Pennsylvania, once a community of Moravians, was named after a story in the Bible. In the Gospel of Luke 24:13-35, we read about an encounter on the road to Emmaus, about seven miles from Jerusalem. This encounter was between Jesus and two of his disciples after the stone had rolled away from Jesus' tomb and he emerged into new life and a new phase of his ministry. The disciples did not recognize Jesus but expressed their sadness about the recent events in Jerusalem. Eating supper with Jesus in Emmaus, they suddenly recognized him when he blessed and broke the bread.

As I took on this new assignment as senior minister of Unity Church of Lehigh Valley in 1994, I came to discover that my role there was the same role Charles and Myrtle Fillmore had more than 100 years earlier—to walk with the good people of this ministry and support them in finding the Christ within themselves and each other.

We spent two delightful and inspiring years in this ministry. The people of Emmaus were warm, congenial, and inspirational. Sadly, our dog, Angel, passed away while we were there.

We were blessed by them and trusted that we, in turn, blessed them.

Threads for Discussion

1. Have you had a "Road to Emmaus" experience where you have walked with someone or were accompanied by companions with whom you shared thoughts, ideas, and spiritual truths that changed your life and the lives of your traveling companions? If so, what transpired as you walked the road together?

2. Have you had a time when you felt that Jesus was walking with you on your path?

3. Do you feel you have physical or spiritual companionship with you on your journey right now?

"HOW 'BOUT THEM COWBOYS!"

Chapter 30

We cannot live only for ourselves. A thousand
fibers connect us with our fellow men; and
among those fibers, as sympathetic threads, our
actions run as causes, and they come back to us as
effects.—Henry Melville

There's a story about the Pope visiting America, and he is invited to Dallas, Texas. At a reception held in his honor, he meets many of the local Texans and finally he is asked to say a few words. Unprepared to speak to these folks of Dallas, he finally agrees. After pausing briefly to gather his thoughts, he shouts, "How 'bout them Cowboys!"

The Pope gets a standing ovation and wins the evening.

One day in Emmaus, Pennsylvania, while reading the latest news from Unity World Headquarters, my eye caught a piece that revealed Unity Church of Dallas was looking for a new minister. Its longtime and extremely popular leader was retiring and they were on the hunt to find a suitable replacement.

I knew extraordinarily little about the Dallas ministry and even less about Dallas itself. However, I did know that this was one of the largest Unity churches in the world, with a congregation nearing 1,000.

I was quite happy in Emmaus, but the lure of the megachurch began speaking loudly to me. I talked it over with Donna, and she agreed we should give it a go. I applied for the job, and within a month or so, the board of directors invited Donna and me to fly to Dallas to try out for the coveted position.

I found that, truly, there is such a thing as Southern hospitality. The people of Dallas were warm, gracious, energetic, and easy to get to know. I spoke on a Sunday and was impressed by the size of the auditorium and how many people filed in to hear my sermon. More than that, the people seemed to "get" my message that Sunday.

After the sermon, Donna and I spent time with the board and members of what turned out to be the largest Unity church staff I had ever encountered. They say that everything is bigger in Texas, and I can believe it!

After my tryout, we returned to Pennsylvania and waited and prayed our prayer and trusted the guiding thread.

We waited and we waited. It seemed like forever before we got a call from the gentleman who was leading the ministerial selection committee in Dallas. He said they had decided on a new minister, but it wasn't me. They chose another gentleman but said I had been "a close second." I asked whom they had chosen, and he told me the man's name. I thanked him for considering me and for their hospitality.

Six months later, almost to the day, I received a call from the same chair of the search committee informing me that the minister they had selected was leaving and they wanted me to be their new minister.

And so we agreed to move to Dallas, Texas, in the spring of 1996. We packed up and, together with our two cats, headed for Big D.

Our time in Dallas was dazzling, inspiring, and challenging. The ministry staff was large and getting larger. Keeping our finger on the pulse of the church was a daunting job. We did, however, make a lot of friends and found ourselves opening to the Texas way of life.

One of the highlights of our time in Dallas was connecting with the Dalai Mamas, a small group of Unity women dedicated to the spiritual and prayer support of other Unity members, their friends, and families. While in Dallas, Donna and I became honorary members and enjoyed times of mutual support, prayer, and abundant laughter.

I even got to go to a Dallas Cowboys game. The team was helpful to me in one way because their Sunday home games always started at 1 p.m. sharp. So I knew I had to make sure that my sermon and the rest of the Sunday service was finished by noon, or I would hear about it! Many of the congregation were Cowboys fans and would be heading to the stadium or home to the television set right after the service.

A most memorable and significant event happened while we were in Dallas. In the year 2002, I had the great honor of ordaining my dear wife as a Unity minister in a special ceremony. Donna was employed by the church and assisted me in ministerial duties, which were many and varied. I have always loved working with her in ministry. She was an inspiration to so many and filled a role in ministry that I could never fill. She was my Myrtle Fillmore in so many ways.

Ever since we met and married in Spokane in 1978, Donna has worked alongside me in various capacities of support as well as initiating her own unique talents and abilities that augmented our ministry together. During our Hawaii ministry, she began taking classes to become a licensed Unity teacher. At the church, she ultimately became the director of our extensive counseling ministry as well as director of our professional music department. Her great joy, however, was leading meditations in the three Sunday services.

Then while we were in Dallas, she took a bold step forward by taking classes over three years to become an ordained Unity minister through a program called field licensing, which allows independent study while actively working in ministry. Donna felt ordination was important not only because of the additional training and stature it would bring, but to equip her for other opportunities in which she could express her gifts. As she continued to work beside me in the Dallas ministry and subsequently the Kailua ministry, she found herself guided into a career in chaplaincy.

After eight amazing years in Texas, leaving behind wonderful friends and great memories, it was time to wish Dallas goodbye and move on.

On to the next chapter!

Threads for Discussion

1. Have you collaborated with a spouse or a partner in a particular project or job? How did that work out?

2. Have you ever had a job that stretched you to your highest level and brought out more of what is within you—more than you ever thought possible? How did that turn out for you?

3. Were you ever a part of a prayer and healing group? If so, what effect did it have?

WHAT? HAWAII CALLS AGAIN?

Chapter 31

Hawaii is not a state of mind but a state of grace.
—Paul Theroux

When I was steaming toward the Hawaiian Islands on the *SS Lakemba* back in 1964, while we were still quite a distance away, I noticed a fragrance filling the air. It was the flowers of Hawaii. I knew I was already "threaded" to the islands. Donna felt the same from a vacation she and her mother enjoyed years earlier.

Donna had this persistent feeling that she had once lived on the island of Kauai in a former life. On one of our visits to the Garden Isle, she took me to the place where she actually felt she was home. She had very strong vibes from this place and remains certain that her threads go back to a time of living in this sacred place.

As we completed our work in Dallas, we learned of a ministerial opening on the windward side of Oahu. On our previous adventure in Hawaii, we had served in Honolulu at Unity Church of Hawaii for eight years.

We knew little about the windward (eastern) side of the island, except for one little patch of beach in the town of Kailua. The beach is known as Lanikai. And it just might be the most beautiful beach in the world, although you may have your own opinion about that. Of all the beaches where Donna and I have walked barefoot through the sand, this was the one that we called Our Beach.

So when the door opened to return to a place we loved, we jumped at the opportunity. Knowing of our work in the Honolulu ministry in previous years, the Kailua Unity community warmly and enthusiastically invited us to join them.

We packed our belongings and headed across the sea—this time by air but with our furniture and stuff taking the slow journey by freighter. We arrived in Honolulu in June 2003. Our two cats, Willy and Gracie, acquired as kittens in Dallas, arrived in the same plane in the cargo hold. They seemed no worse for wear after their eight-hour trip from Dallas. We were glad to learn that animals no longer had to be in quarantine, so we were able to take them with us directly to our new home.

And so here we were—returning to the islands once again. We were greeted with flower leis by the president of the church board and his wife, who, it turned out, were to become our landlord and lady. They had a house to rent in Kailua and offered it to us at a very reasonable rent. Unity Windward church, we were to discover, shared a beautiful church building with the Seventh-day Adventist Church. It was a friendly and amicable relationship. We were able to have space during the week for our offices and for classes. And since the Adventists had services on Saturday, Sunday was all ours.

Earlier, I mentioned a trio of traveling troubadours who had led Donna, me, and about three dozen members of the Northwest Adults of Unity on retreat in Menucha, Washington, back in 1979. They had introduced us to what was to become a key part of our spiritual study—A Course in Miracles. Now ministering in Kailua, we were thrilled to welcome a member of that trio to sing for us and lead a workshop on a Sunday in 2004. His name was Charley Thweatt, one of the original trio.

I remember well one of the songs he sang that Sunday was called "You're an Angel!"

To hear this angel of a man sing this song touched me deeply, but not nearly as much as it did for Donna. It was as though the guiding thread was singing directly to and through her, introducing her to and guiding her where her own spiritual thread would lead in the days, months, and years ahead.

Within a few days, Donna inquired about a hospital chaplaincy training program in Honolulu. Without hesitation and with clear guidance, she decided to sign up for it and was soon joined by other trainees working in the hospital system throughout the island of Oahu.

Instantly, she knew she had found her calling and a sacred space she could fill, using her many talents and Unity background. She enjoyed her new ministry so much that she stayed in the training program to its completion and became certified to serve as a hospital chaplain. Here, emerging, was another of the healing threads that was to embrace Donna's life and career until this very day. More on this later.

On our days off, especially early in the mornings before the sun came up, we would drive the short distance from our little house on Hui Street to find a parking spot near one of the public walkways to Lanikai Beach. There was always a warm, inviting breeze that welcomed us as we walked along a palm-lined path to the beach. We could hear the surf coming onshore from some distance away.

Once the beach came into view, the first thing we looked for were the two small islands about a mile offshore. These are known as the Mokulua Islands or just "The Mokes" for short. We would take our places on some large stones on the beach or claim a beach chair or two that had been left behind. The morning show consisted of watching the sun rise over the eastern horizon. The sunrises were always spectacular, and we could feel the connection with all of creation and especially with the gift that the guiding thread was offering. We would never grow tired of this inspiring way to begin our day and find new strength for the tasks at hand. We spent a memorable and inspiring seven years in Kailua and loved every minute of it.

But, once again, there was another compelling thread that began tugging at us.

Threads for Discussion ————————————————————————————

1. What would be your picture of a perfect paradise? Do you have a place on the planet where you have visited that you would call paradise?

2. How often did you visit there? What was it about this place that lifted you and inspired you?

3. Do you have plans to return there?

4. Is there an event or experience that helped you find your calling or directed you toward a new path for your life?

THE THREADS WIND BACK TO SPOKANE
Chapter 32

We leave something of ourselves behind when we leave a place, we stay there, even though we go away. And there are things in us that we can find again only by going back there. —Pascal Mercier, *Night Train to Lisbon*

As much as we loved Hawaii, the thread pulling us now was called "home" and it was pointing us to Spokane—back to the place where we met, married, and marveled at each other. Another key motivation was finances. Prices in Hawaii were beyond anything we had ever experienced before, and we knew we would have to make a change.

But the main tug we felt was Donna's mother back in Spokane. Concern and care for her would eventually draw us back to our old stomping grounds. This was the woman with all the connections to the early beginnings of the Church of Truth, then Unity Church of Truth, and one of the key figures in helping develop the new church building on Bernard on the South Hill. This was the woman who agreed to take my place on the escorted trip to Australia and New Zealand back in 1976. This was the woman who gave birth to the one who would become my soulmate and life partner.

Her health was beginning to wane, and it was becoming clear she needed more support and assistance. Donna became quite concerned about her, so in 2009 we agreed to say *aloha* once again to the islands and head for the Pacific Northwest.

We found an apartment in the same complex as Donna's mother, which worked out beautifully for being able to visit her quickly and often and take her to medical appointments, to shopping, and to church. She so appreciated our returning to Spokane, and we were beginning to feel this might very well be our home for the rest of our lives.

Meanwhile, returning to Unity Church of Truth on Bernard as congregants, we reacquainted ourselves with senior minister

Clare Austen, the young woman we had met at the Young Adults of Unity Conference back in 1976 at Menucha. She had the church growing and thriving, and there came a point when she decided she needed some ministerial assistance with this fast-growing congregation. She asked whether I would be interested in coming on board as an associate minister. I had intended to retire and simply offer my support and services as needed. The thread had other ideas. Since I knew the ministry well and had many friends and contacts there, it seemed like a good fit, so once again I put on my ministerial cap and took the job.

Donna also had intended to retire or at best to volunteer her services wherever needed. However, now trained as a hospital chaplain, she was drawn to the chaplaincy ministry at the largest hospital in the Inland Empire, Sacred Heart Medical Center. She wanted something to fill and fulfill her days and felt she might volunteer her services there.

She made an appointment with a senior chaplain and offered to work as a volunteer. She was startled when the man said to her, "Wouldn't you like to get paid for your services?" Donna was stunned. She said, "Why, yes, of course!" And within a few days she was hired as a supplemental chaplain.

And so, once again, the healing thread of Donna's ancestors, and the healing ministry of Myrtle Fillmore, and the guiding ministry of Charles Fillmore pulled her back into a life of service.

To this day, as I write these words, she walks the halls of Sacred Heart, uplifting patients, praying with those with healing challenges, and standing by in times of trouble and tragedy. She is well-known by many on the hospital staff and beloved by everyone. Aside from a slight departure from her chaplaincy ministry when she was ill, she continues to be a beacon of light to everyone she meets.

In 2012, Clare Austen announced she was retiring as minister at Unity Church of Truth. She asked me whether I would be willing to stay on as senior minister once again. I decided to give it a go and said *yes* once more!

A lot had changed in almost two decades since I had walked the hallowed halls of this amazing place. But with the help of a great staff, wonderful volunteers, and an enthusiastic and responsive congregation, we forged ahead. Charles and Myrtle's legacy and their unifying threads continued. You already know what lay in store, however. Another thread—one not so friendly—was about to reveal itself in and through my life. I was about to see how all my fun in the sun—over the years of my childhood, then in Australia and Hawaii—had impacted my body and my world. But the healing threads of Myrtle and Charles Fillmore touched my heart, mind, and body and restored me to wholeness.

Threads for Discussion

1. Have you ever gone back to a place where you lived for many years? How did you find things? How did you react and respond to what you found there?

2. Did new opportunities open for you, or did you find most of the doors had closed since you left?

3. What was your overall feeling of returning "home"? Whose home was it, your parents' or one where you and others lived?

4. What did you learn about yourself through this experience?

5. Have you called upon and aligned yourself with the guiding thread?

THE THREADS CONTINUE

Chapter 33

*It was perfectly normal for the people like Charles
and Myrtle Fillmore to ask, as did Emerson, "Why
can we not have a firsthand experience of God?"*
—Eric Butterworth

Just as the Fillmores looked back for that thread of spiritual
continuity that joined them with healing, Donna and I found
ourselves looking back to our connection, not only to the
Fillmores, but still further back to all those who are part of the
unending thread of individuals who have sought and found the
original thread.

And just as the Fillmores and those who came before and
after them have sought to follow that connection to expand their
awareness into the future, Donna and I, looking forward now,
continue to see more and more evidence of this thread ahead of
us and beyond.

With our lives solidly built on Myrtle's healing discovery (*I am
a child of God, and therefore I do not inherit sickness*) plus further
being open and willing to seek guidance from what Charles called
"headquarters" (our version being *Here am I, Lord. Use me.*),
we continue to spend each day still seeking, still learning, still
trusting that our way is guided by what we have come to know as
One Presence and One Power, God the Good, Omnipotent.

Though the age of our bodies increases each day, we continue
to meet and greet each day with the same spirit that Charles
Fillmore articulated at the age of 93. He expressed his passion
for life by affirming: *I fairly sizzle with zeal and enthusiasm and
spring forth with a mighty faith to do the things that ought to be
done by me.*

Some days, we both admit, there's more fizzle than sizzle. But
we keep on keeping on.

And so, as we both continue to extend these unifying threads
into the days and months to come, we invite you to trace the

threads that reveal themselves in your life. We invite you to be ready and willing to embrace and claim them as your own.

This is the purpose of writing this book. Just as our lives have been so blessed, so guided, and so full, and just as we have found so many instances where threads have revealed themselves to us, we are affirming that they also live and move and have their being in and through you. Right here and right now.

The tapestry in anyone's life is never finished, though there are times when it seems to be set aside for a while. But if there's anything Donna and I have learned about the healing and guiding threads, it is that when called upon, they will always deliver. There's more healing within you and available to you than you can ever comprehend.

Even when you think you've come to the end of a relationship, the end of the game, or a diagnosis threatens to bring your life to a screeching halt, just hold to the Truth that you are a child of the healing, guiding threads and you inherit health and wholeness.

And that, dear friend, is what Donna and I know about you. Of this you can be certain.

ACKNOWLEDGMENTS

I wish to acknowledge the physicians and their staff whose wisdom, skill, compassion, and support contributed significantly to my healing and to the writing of this book:

Christopher Lee, M.D., Radiologist

Brian Mitchell, D.O., Otolaryngologist

Peter Schlegel, M.D., Oncologist

Julie Ulloa-Michaelis, M.D.

The Staff at Cancer Care Northwest, Spokane

ABOUT THE AUTHOR

David W. McClure has been a Unity minister for more than 60 years. He was introduced to the principles of Unity and New Thought at the age of 7 by his mother, who found a Unity church in their hometown of Toronto so that she and other family members could learn more about modern New Thought.

David graduated from Unity Sunday School, the Youth of Unity, and eventually entered the ministerial program under the leadership of James Dillet Freeman in 1960. He has served in ministries in Vancouver, Australia, New Zealand, Iowa, California, Washington state, Hawaii, Pennsylvania, and Texas.

David served as president of the Association of Unity Churches in 1980. In 2016, he received the Charles Fillmore Award, which is given to honor a Unity minister for special contributions toward the work of the Fillmores.

His wife, Donna, also an ordained Unity minister, is currently serving as a hospital chaplain in Spokane, Washington. You will often find her in one of these departments: Cardiac Intensive Care, ICU, Neonatal ICU, Surgery, Dialysis, Oncology, Emergency, or wherever she is needed.

The McClures continue to serve the One Presence and One Power wherever the unifying thread takes them.